FIERCE
AUTHENTICITY

FIERCE
AUTHENTICITY

SHOW UP.
BE **SEEN**.
GET LOVE.

Shirani M. Pathak

CONTENTS

This book is dedicated

to all those who have gone before me,

and all those who will come after me.

♥

*One day, in retrospect, the years of struggle
will strike you as the most beautiful.*

—Sigmund Freud

INTRODUCTION

I'm going to let you in on a little secret: Love always surrounds you and is constantly seeking a way into your life. It's there, waiting for you. Like a lost little puppy dog desiring to be cuddled, eagerly seeking you out, craving for you to welcome it in, love is there. Waiting for you to see it, waiting for you to acknowledge it, waiting for you to invite it in. Love is just as available to you as the air you breathe, in quantities as vast as the stars in the night sky.

The problem is, you can't see it. You walk around with blinders on, looking for love in all the wrong places, all the while living behind walls built so high that you have no idea love is on the other side, waiting to be let in. You have too many stories and beliefs about yourself to let love in. Somewhere along the way, you created stories about how unlovable, undesirable, and unwanted you must be. Deep down inside, you fear that "if you really knew me, you wouldn't like me, and you sure as hell wouldn't love me." You walk around hiding behind masks, knowing exactly which mask to bring out for which situation or interaction, while trying so hard to hold the fragile pieces of yourself together.

You're tired. You feel disconnected. You feel isolated at times, and if you're honest with yourself, you sometimes feel pretty alone, too. You could be with your closest friends, or even your partner, and still get the sense you're all alone. Sure, you might be close to people—you might even already have found the love of your life, and at the same time, you could be keeping them at arm's length, keeping them from truly getting to know who you are.

You want so badly to be loved, but you always seem to pick lovers who can't love you back. And when you do find a lover who loves you back, you find them boring. You do something stupid to fuck it up.

In the beginning, you're both filled with desire and the passion is hot. Then, just when the relationship starts to deepen, it starts to fail. One of you either goes MIA, completely ghosting the other, or one of you changes. They stop showering you with the attention and affection they did before they slept with you, or you do the same to them.

If you're the one who got left, you do everything in your

power to draw them back to you. You de-prioritize your friends, you stop taking care of you, and you make the one you lost your everything, sitting around waiting for a text or call. When they don't reciprocate, you try harder, and harder, and harder, bending yourself into pretzels to get them to love you again. When you finally realize it's done, that your lover is gone and isn't coming back, you spiral into the rabbit hole of the not-enoughs: I must not have been pretty enough, thin enough, funny enough, smart enough, witty enough, sexy enough ... because if I was, they would still be here with me; they didn't stay, which simply goes to prove that I am not enough.

If you're the one who got bored, you start to pull away. You get annoyed when your partner seems to get clingy. You push them further and further away, until either you finally break it off or they've had enough and call it quits with you. At first you feel free. Then, after some time has passed, you realize that you miss them and that you might have fucked it up. You reach out and you're hurt when they want nothing to do with you. That's when you start to go into your not-enoughs: I must not be lovable enough, worthy enough, skilled enough, sexy enough, charming enough ... because if I was, they would have come back; they didn't, so how bad I suck is confirmed once again.

Whether you were left or did the leaving, your

not-enoughness meter has been turned up to high. You turn to your friends, and to ice cream, brownies, cookies, wine, and as many self-help books as you can find. You have an insatiable hunger to be loved, and you turn your obsession with your lost love into an obsession about everything that's wrong with you. If you could just fix yourself, you could go out there and get the love you so badly desire.

If any of this sounds familiar, then welcome. I'm so glad you're here.

I know how it feels to bend myself into a pretzel to get someone to like me. I know how it feels to put the lovers in my life before my family and friends. I know how it feels to walk around constantly juggling all the different masks so no one gets to know the real me and discover how unlovable I believe myself to be.

It's a terribly painful and lonely place to be.

Just like you, I used to question what was wrong with me. Why did lovers never stay? When I had a good guy, why did I always push him away? I had no idea, so I became a seeker, a searcher, and a learner. I sought out therapy, self-help books, 12-step programs, workshops, and more self-help books. I was a high-functioning, overachieving doer. I needed to know what was wrong with me so I could fix it. I was determined to figure it out so I could feel better.

Then one day it hit me: *I* was the one common denominator in all my failed relationships. The problem was me. It wasn't about *them*. It was about me. Much to my surprise, though, by digging in and doing the work, I learned there wasn't anything actually wrong with me. I had simply developed some very wrong beliefs about myself. Those false and erroneous beliefs led me to act in ways that took me out of integrity with myself, led me to de-prioritize myself, and ultimately, led me to abandon myself time and time again.

As a relationship therapist on my own healing path, it never ceased to amaze me that every woman who showed up on my couch, whether she was single, married, or something in-between, was a woman walking through the same experiences as me. Because I am a seeker and a searcher and a lifelong learner, I took everything I had learned on my own personal and professional journey and began to apply the principles and theories with my clients and others I mentored.

What I found was that every single woman who struggled with her relationships had stories about her enoughness. Stories she developed in her early years were unconsciously running the script of her entire life. She had the same few scenes on repeat, as though they were reruns of the same familiar Friday night sitcom. The people were different and some of the details in the scene might change, but her feelings were always the same: She was not-enough and she was unworthy of love and affection.

By applying what I had discovered in my own healing journey to the women I worked with, I was able to help them uncover their own stories. We discovered the experiences that led them to create these stories about themselves. We developed the deepest and most-intimate relationship a woman will ever have in her life: the relationship she has with herself. Time and time again, as each woman worked through her stories, the blocks she had stacked against allowing love into her life were slowly removed. Piece by piece, the stories that kept her isolated and walled off, protected but not connected, came down. Revealed behind them was a woman who stood tall in the truth of who she was, knowing that she was a lovable, valuable, worthy human being.

The woman who emerged from behind those walls had developed an unwavering love for herself. She used that newly rediscovered love for herself as the compass to navigate her entire life, and she did so with dignity and grace. Each woman learned that if she allows herself to show up and be seen in the fullness of who she is, she gets to experience a love she never knew was possible.

That's what the process of **fierce authenticity**, and this book, is all about. It's about how to engage in the practice of being fiercely authentic to yourself, so you, too, can allow yourself to show up, be seen, and get the love you've always desired.

This book is based on my own story and the stories of women I have supported in their own process of healing, awakening, and personal evolution. Whether you are in a relationship, single, married, engaged, or in a different type of arrangement, you will find something in here for you. It's best to read this book from cover to cover, in sequence, because each part of the process builds upon the one previous to it. The practice of fierce authenticity is a multipart process that includes fierce love for yourself, fierce care of yourself, and being fiercely and authentically you, and culminates in fierce communication of everything that came before it.

You'll find stories, ideas, and concepts, some spiritual in nature, some based on the latest research on relationships, and many combining the two. They're meant to help you understand your own stories—how they get activated in your life and lead you to sabotage yourself and your relationships. You'll learn what you can do to become intimately familiar with them so they no longer dictate your life and keep you hidden behind walls that keep love out.

If you want to take the practice even deeper and are ready to welcome personalized support, you can learn more at my website, www.ShiraniMPathak.com.

I've also created some awesome bonus meditations and challenges for you that will take what you learn here and expand your practice further. You can download those bonuses at www.fierceauthenticity.com.

I have worked through and continue to practice everything I share with you in this book. I've discovered that every single time I allow myself to show up and be seen, I always get to experience a love that is beyond my wildest dreams. I am so excited for you to dive in and discover how you can cultivate the practice of fierce authenticity in your own life so that you can experience the same! ♥

1

THE PRACTICE OF FIERCE AUTHENTICITY

Fierce Authenticity: The practice of living and loving in a way that allows you to show up, be seen, and get the love you've always wanted.

There was a time in my life when pain and heartache were a regular part of my experience. I was totally boy-crazy—and I always managed to find all the wrong boys. The thrill and the rush of a new crush excited me. Do they love me? Do they love me not? It was like Russian roulette: You never knew what you would get.

Sadly for me, it was always love me not. Every single time I realized it was love me not, I would crash into a spiral of despair. While I was in the chase, excitement and anxiety ruled my experience. When he dumped me, I fell into depression … until another him came along.

As for the ones who were actually good guys, they weren't even on my radar. They already liked me. Where was the drama and the excitement in that? No thrilling push-pull, no do they love me or do they love me not. They were boring. No, thank you. And so it continued. The funny thing is, I wanted so badly to be married and have a family one day. Too bad my choices in partners didn't reflect that desire.

Little did I know at that time in my life that although part of me really did want partnership and connection, another part of me was operating based on unconscious scripts and stories I had about my own ability to be loved, my own not-enoughness, and a deep-rooted fear that to love and be loved is dangerous and unsafe. Thankfully, around the age of 27, I had a heartbreak that finally led me to seek answers to what was really going on with me.

The concepts and ideas I share with you in this book are the synthesis of what I learned along the way. As a therapist and a healer, I took what I learned through my own personal and professional journey and began teaching it to clients. Lo and behold, what had been working for me also directly applied to and worked with my clients. Then it worked with workshop participants. And then it worked with other professionals when I was invited to share about this work in their workplaces. Somewhere along the way, the practice of **fierce authenticity** was born.

WIRED FOR CONNECTION

We humans have a high tolerance for pain in our lives. We're also wired for connection. It's usually the pain of our romantic partnerships, or our lack thereof, that leads us to the breaking point. We all want to love and be loved back. When we aren't experiencing that in our lives, we realize something must change. When I realized I was the common denominator in all my failed and painful relationships, I was ready for change. I hope you're ready to experience change in your life and relationships as well.

The practice of fierce authenticity may seem to apply only to romantic relationships, but it goes beyond that. Fierce authenticity is about how you carry yourself through the world. Psychological research supports the idea that your relationships are directly related to and based upon how you feel about yourself. If you're anything like me, a perfectionist and overachiever, then you likely end up navigating your world and your relationships from a place of lack. By lack I mean all of the not-enoughs: not good enough, pretty enough, smart enough, accomplished enough—the list goes on. The not-enoughs are based on the stories you developed about yourself as a result of painful childhood experiences. Stories of not-enoughness underlie your unfulfilling relationships.

Fierce authenticity is a manner of living and loving in an authentic, present, wholehearted way, free from the pain of the stories and limitations that have held you back. It doesn't mean you no longer have your stories of pain and suffering. It means you no longer allow those stories to dictate your day-to-day experience.

When you are living and loving in a fiercely authentic way, you feel a sense of peace. You feel grounded. You feel whole. Your old stories no longer have power over you. The things which once caused great struggle and strife in your life no longer upset you in the ways they used to. You have the ability to see when others are operating from their own stories of pain and suffering, and you don't take their words or their actions personally. You instead love them in a deeply, fiercely authentic way.

That said, fierce authenticity doesn't mean you fall into a codependent, people-pleasing, bending-over-backward-for-other-people pattern. Quite the opposite: When you're fiercely authentic, your boundaries get even stronger. You learn to let others live the lives they're meant to live, while taking care of yourself in the process.

This is not to say that hurt and discomfort won't ever come up for you. You won't live like an enlightened guru, with nothing fazing you. Nope; not at all. What it does mean is when something comes up, you have the ability to check in with yourself, evaluate what is being stirred up within you, and then decide rationally how to proceed.

In workshops and private sessions with clients, I often say that it's about noticing where things get sticky in you. It's like Velcro: If there's nothing for the yuckiness to stick to, it won't. It will just keep on moving. If there is something for it to stick to, your task is to connect with yourself and evaluate what's arising for healing within you. I like to remind people of the childhood saying, "I'm rubber, you're glue; what bounces off me, sticks to you." What makes one person rubber and one person glue in certain situations? Our stories and how much we have done to heal them.

FIERCE AUTHENTICITY AS A PRACTICE

Fierce authenticity is a process of transformation. It is a practice that will take you deep into the depths of your heart and soul, and crack you wide open, so your heart can expand and allow you to experience the love you were born to experience.

Sandra's story illustrates what transformation can look like. As you read her story, notice any thoughts or feelings that feel familiar. Looking for the similarities and appreciating the differences helps make the practice of fierce authenticity stronger.

Sandra is a 36-year-old marketing executive. She tended to get into relationships with men who would be interested in her for a couple of months, and then *poof,* disappear into thin air. She couldn't understand what was happening. Her career was going well, she had great friends in her life, and she was in regular communication with her family. She held onto anger and bitterness, and the wall she had built around herself became clearly noticeable.

Our work began following yet another one of these instances in which a romantic interest whose company she enjoyed had disappeared on her.

"I just don't understand!" she exclaimed. "We were really into each other, he said he really enjoyed our time together, and then he just disappeared! He stopped returning my texts, didn't answer my calls. He ghosted me. What the fuck?"

Her confusion was very real, and yet I knew the problem from the moment she called. Sandra was an overachiever, accustomed to hustling for her value so she could prove herself worthy of love and affection. She brought this same hustle to her romantic relationships.

Through our work together, Sandra was able to identify a family pattern. Her dad worked endlessly and was almost never home; her mom's attention was divided among all the household responsibilities, the kids, and her own job. Sandra thought that to win her parents' approval, she had to do more, be more, and achieve more, so she hustled as hard as she could. That's how she had done so well in school. That's how she got all straight As and honors. That's how she graduated *summa cum laude* in college and how she landed the dream job where she was kicking ass. Sandra's hustle had served her well in many ways.

Sandra discovered that she brought the same hustle to her romantic relationships. When we explored even deeper, she realized she brought the same hustle to her friendships and her work. After so many years of hustling, she was tired. She was burnt out. She was stressed out. She was about to fall apart, yet she was holding it together because that's what over-functioners do.

Sandra learned that as a young girl, she had made up a story about herself: The only way for me to get love is to prove myself worthy of it. As a little girl, Sandra subconsciously realized her parents prioritized education, work, and achievements. Her mind made up the meaning that getting those things was the golden ticket to getting love. As a young girl, Sandra sought love through academics. As an adult, she sought it through work.

Sandra came to this powerful awareness by practicing fierce authenticity. When she did, her life took a whole new direction. Through the acts of loving herself, caring for herself, and getting to know herself authentically as she is, Sandra was able to communicate with love, care, and a level of authenticity so fierce that nothing and no one could tear her down. As Sandra allowed herself to be authentic in all aspects of her life, she let her walls come down and others see her as the bright and beautiful being she was. From that point forward, her friendships were more nourishing; her career, which had been starting to feel stale and unfulfilling, catapulted to new heights. Her life had more meaning. She felt confident in her interactions, not only in the dating world but the world in general.

Sandra also noticed that things that once bothered her—things that used to stick to her like glue—no longer did. When something did stick to her, she now saw it as an invitation to get curious and heal a deeper layer.

By the time Sandra and I finished our work together, she was completely transformed. The woman who had a fragile sense of self and was barely holding it together was now only a memory. The woman who walked out the door carried herself with confidence, navigated challenges in life with dignity and grace, and fully understood the depth of her own lovability. Sandra was living and loving fierce authenticity in all areas of her life.

Sandra's story isn't unique. I stand before you as a woman who has walked through the process of fierce authenticity and now practice it in my life daily. Sandra's transformation is possible for you, too. It starts with one simple question: How do you want to feel in your life?

As you ask yourself the question, notice what images, words, or feelings arise for you. There's no need to judge what arises or to feel anything arise at all. Simply know that as you learn more about the practice of fierce authenticity, you will receive greater clarity about how it applies to you.

One cool psychological factoid is that our minds don't know the difference between what's real and what's imagined. When you are able to imagine the way you want to feel with your mind, body, and soul, it becomes much closer to reality for you. When you have examples like Sandra, it becomes easier to believe that what's possible for someone else is possible for you, too.

COMMIT TO HONORING YOURSELF

Fierce authenticity is about living and loving in a way that is uniquely you. It comes from being deeply aligned with who you are by freeing yourself from all of the false stories and beliefs you were ever told, or told yourself, about yourself throughout your life. To reach that alignment, you're going to have to do your part. The Universe operates in a mysterious and magical way. When you decide to work on yourself and heal whatever gets in the way of you being the full expression of yourself, every single block and barrier you have will come up and make itself known to you.

I like to compare it to a process of detox. When you make the decision to say yes to you, the entire Universe co-conspires to ensure that everything that isn't you arises to be released. Through this process of detoxification, your false beliefs arise to be healed, leaving the true and authentic version of you.

The practice of fierce authenticity means unlearning most of what you thought you knew about yourself. It's a process of deconditioning all of your prior conditioning. It will require you to take a journey deep into your mind, body, and soul. You'll discover what your stories are, where they came from, and whether these stories even want to be a part of your reality today. It's challenging work that will require your utmost dedication and commitment, but don't worry. I've broken this book down into simple, bite-sized pieces so you can start to experience living in a fiercely authentic way.

Don't get me wrong. I've broken the practice down into simple steps, but they still require effort from you. As with anything in life, you are absolutely responsible for your own healing and well-being. You are the sole person responsible for how this practice works for you.

Before we go any further, I want you to make a commitment to yourself: No matter how hard this gets, and no matter how uncomfortable it might feel at times, you will stay with your process. I promise that if you do this work, your life will begin to change in miraculous ways. Take a moment, place your hand on your heart, close your eyes (if that feels right), take a deep breath, and say this:

> *I, [state your full name], make a commitment
> to honoring myself. Honoring myself means
> I will learn to cultivate a deeply nourishing
> relationship with myself, based on love, care,
> and authenticity, so I can navigate the world
> as my true, fiercely authentic self. As I do
> this, I will experience the miracles, flow, and
> ease life has in store for me. I am ready. It's*

my time to show up, be seen, and get love. I
am ready to release and receive. ♥

Once you state your commitment to yourself, pause for a moment and feel the power of your words moving through you. Breathe in and out, and simply allow. Intention-setting is a powerful tool. By proclaiming your commitment to honoring yourself, you have already taken your endeavor to the next level.

BUILDING YOUR FOUNDATION

Learning to cultivate and nourish a deeply wholesome and fulfilling relationship with yourself through the practice of fierce authenticity is a four-part process, with a series of little steps along the way. These parts of the process are the most-important building blocks of any relationship. Without them, your foundation for experiencing fulfilling relationships with yourself and others will be shaky and wobbly, as though it was built on sand.

The four foundational steps build upon one another. In order, they are: Fierce Love (for yourself), Fierce Care (of yourself), Fierce Authenticity, and Fierce Communication.

Loving ourselves means caring for ourselves, and caring for ourselves means being authentic with ourselves and others. When we do all of these things combined, we are able to communicate with a fierce level of love, care, and authenticity with ourselves and others in our lives.

Fierce love (for ourselves) is the premise that we must first love ourselves to be able to love others. If we don't have love for ourselves, how can we possibly give love to others?

This builds up to the second part of the process, **fierce care** (of yourself). You can't pour from an empty cup. If your self-care cup is empty, you have no care or consideration to give others—just like the step on love: You can't give what you don't have.

Once you have taken the time to cultivate love and care for yourself in your life, you will then be able to work on **fierce authenticity**. Fierce authenticity is the premise that once you love yourself and care for yourself, you can learn who you really, truly, authentically are.

Once you know who you authentically are, without the stories and the labels others have given you, then you can **communicate** with others in a way that allows you to show up, be seen, and get love. The entire process and what you can experience at each stage of the process, is really quite magical. And it feels oh, so good!

At this point, some of you might be thinking, "Wait a minute! I thought relationships are built on love, trust, and safety?" You're absolutely right! They are. But safety and trust come from within. Once you've developed a loving and nurturing relationship with yourself, you will have established a sense of safety, and therefore trust, from within. With that sense of safety and trust, you'll be able to navigate the world, trusting yourself to know who's safe and who isn't. Rather than choosing to be in relationship with people, places, and things that used to make parts of you feel unsettled, you'll trust your own inner knowing. Ultimately, that's what fierce authenticity is all about.

NO WOMAN IS AN ISLAND

Learning the practice of fierce authenticity is going to require some effort on your part. There might be times where things get hard and you might feel like giving up. You also might find some really uncomfortable things arise for you. I know, because it happened to me. When I was deep in my healing I can't even remember how many times I said to myself, "Fuck this shit! I give up!" It was in those times that my mentors, my therapist, my sponsor, my coaches, and my friends were even more instrumental and necessary in my life. Without them, I would have given up. Had we all given up, we wouldn't have gotten to the truth about ourselves— the truth of our beauty, our brilliance, and our inherent worthiness, simply because we exist. We wouldn't have been able to experience true peace and true joy in our lives.

We wouldn't have been able to carry ourselves through the world based on authentic alignment with who we are and what we are here to do. We wouldn't have learned how to suit up, show up, and get love.

Every single person I have ever supported through the practice of fierce authenticity is now experiencing a great big life filled with so much love, happiness, fulfillment, and joy.

Don't fall into the trap of giving up. This is powerful work. With every fiber of my being, I want you to make it to the other side so you too can experience the miracles of fierce authenticity.

You will probably need support along this journey. No person is an island—we're not meant to do this alone. Find yourself an accountability buddy, a mentor, a therapist, a sponsor, a coach, or a friend who can be with you and support you on this wild ride of discovering yourself. It might get messy, and that's all part of the process.

Take a moment right now to consider who your support people are and what you can do if the practice of cultivating fierce authenticity becomes overwhelming. Also ask yourself, how can you keep yourself accountable to your healing? Then reach out to your people and let them know you are about to step into deep exploration as you learn about the practice of fierce authenticity. If you need ideas or suggestions, please see the Further Resources section at the back of the book.

RELATIONAL ANATOMY

Before we delve any deeper into the process of fierce authenticity and how you can begin to show up, be seen, and get love in your life, it's important for you to learn a few key points about your relational anatomy. Relational anatomy contributes to how you operate in your relationships. Your relational anatomy informs your relationships and your patterns of relating. Learning the basics of relational anatomy sets the groundwork for your foundation of living and loving through the practice of fierce authenticity. Understanding what your relationship patterns have been and where they came from will help you as you go through the practice. Similarly to building a house, you must first prep the ground.

Every single one of us moves through life with different stories we have about ourselves. My stories, similar to most of the people I have worked with, included "I must not be lovable" and "To be loved, I have to prove myself worthy of it." For years, I didn't even realize these were the stories operating in my life. I would have experience after experience that reiterated my belief about my unlovability.

I seriously felt angry about my hand in life, the unfairness of my family, my romantic relationships, my bosses, God—*everyone.* I carried myself with a feeling of discontent deep within my body and being. And here's the kicker: I didn't even know it!

I simply thought life was unfair and God didn't love me. Little did I know that I was operating from a place of unconscious beliefs about myself, which I was playing out and calling fate.

Similarly to many people I have worked with, the one area of my life where I did well was academics. This was something I could have control over. My family valued education and achievements. I learned that the way to winning the love and approval of my family was through academics and then career achievements. As I got older and made my way through high school (with all honors and AP classes, by the way—true overachiever here) and then college, I would get so excited about my grades and share them with my parents, only to hear, "You only got an A? Why not an A+?" My GPA in high school was *over* 4.0, and my family would still ask, "Why not an A+?"

Thankfully, there came a point where I was able to recognize that grades were my family's stuff, not mine. I didn't have to add my grades to the list of stories about how badly I sucked (I had enough of those anyway).

Although I did well academically and had a pretty good group of friends, I found myself with the nagging feeling that I wasn't enough. I didn't know it at the time, but stories I learned very early on kept me feeling as if there was something wrong with me. Where do these not-enoughs come from?

Relational anatomy is comprised of three parts: the relational hurts and wounds you experienced in your early relationships; the stress, drama, and chaos you create in your life as a response to your early relational hurts; and the relational mirrors who show you how you are playing out your early wounds. Your relational anatomy will help you uncover where your not-enoughs come from.

The Wound

The moment in which you learn or develop the story of your not-enoughness is what I call the wound. Wounds of not-enoughness occur in relationships. The moment you have an experience that you don't understand, based on how the adults or others around you respond, you make up a story about what it means—and not only what it means in general, but what it means about *you*. When the story is you were not protected, loved, cherished, celebrated, understood, your mind makes up the meaning that you are *not worthy* of being protected, loved, cherished, celebrated, and understood, because if you were, the adults around you would have treated you so.

The wound doesn't have to be a big, traumatic experience such as the death of a loved one, divorce, or abuse. It can be as simple as being excited about an art project and your parent not meeting your excitement about it due to their own preoccupation with something else. Overtime, a collection of relational wounds, if left untended, can become the basis of some of your most-erroneous stories about yourself.

According to classic psychology, children are highly egocentric, meaning they're self-centered, and believe the world revolves around them. Using that lens, when a child has an experience, even if it has nothing to do with them, they make up a story about themselves. The human mind needs to make meaning, and it does so via story. That's why even when an event has nothing to do with us, we make it mean something about ourselves.

Although we humans have minds that seek to make meaning, we are also animals. As with other animals, when wounded, we do everything we can to hide that we have been wounded and we find ways to work around the wound.

If you've ever seen a hurt animal, you know that when

they've been hurt, they often don't let on to the fact. Your puppy may have gotten a thorn in his paw, and he probably isn't going to let you know he's been wounded. Instead, he's probably going to become sullen, withdrawn, and protective of the wounded area. You might notice him licking his paw to get some relief, and you'll also notice that if you attempt to approach his paw, he will vigorously protect it, possibly even becoming aggressive and nipping you in the process. Over time, the thorn in his paw will either get infected or heal, or your pup will learn to navigate his world by compensating for the wound. We humans are no different; we do the exact same thing, only we do it mentally and psychically with our relational wounds.

That said, the opposite is true, too. You can also have a painful experience, and the adults in your life are able to meet your needs with the level of love and compassion you need in that moment. Sometimes, the thorn can be lovingly removed and heal over well. In that case, stories of wound become stories of love and healing and are no longer on your radar. However, my focus in this book is to help you learn to address the stories that weren't met with the level of love and presence that you needed in just the exact way you needed it—those are the experiences that become our wounds.

When we have been wounded, we do our best to hide

that we've been hurt. Unfortunately for most of us, that means we shut ourselves off to the potential of any further hurt by closing parts of ourselves off from relationships. We go into withdrawal, start to pull away from family and friends, become quiet and sullen. Others might ask what's wrong and we won't share what's going on with anyone. We learn to suffer in silence. We put on a smile on our face and pretend everything's okay on the outside, but on the inside, we have put up walls to protect us from getting hurt again.

Eventually, similarly to the puppy, we will do our best to keep others away from the parts of us that have been hurt. We will vigorously protect our wounds—even from ourselves—going into deep inner isolation and denial, all the while feeling more and more empty inside. We adapt. Over time, we learn ways to navigate through the world by working around our wound. Usually by the time we reach that point, we're also operating behind walls so tall and so thick that we no longer have access to these hurt and wounded parts of ourselves. Therein lies the true danger of leaving our relational wounds untended.

Our brains and our bodies learn to adapt and we get accustomed to maneuvering around the wound. The funny thing is, sometimes when the wound has been healed and is no longer present, parts of us might feel confused. Parts of us might even start to freak out when there's something missing that's been a part of us for so long. As you progress on your own healing journey, know that there might be times when parts of you start to freak out as well.

Stress, Drama, and Chaos

The stories we make up about ourselves are wildly creative. They follow a sequence:

> Event or experience → your interpretation about the event or experience → your wound from the experience.

That said, not every bad experience becomes a painful, unhealed wound. A wound can't fester when it's met with love and kindness in a way that helps us to feel heard and loved. If you had a painful experience in the past and the adults in your life were able to meet you with love, kindness, compassion, and understanding, in a way that helped you feel cared for and loved, you are likely to overcome the wound. You might realize that a painful thing happened, but you're still loved and cared for and understood.

Most of us have far more positive experiences than negative ones. Because of the way the human brain is wired, however, it's sometimes difficult to remember the good times. The human mind tends to focus on what's painful, rather than what's joyful.

My sister is four years younger than I am. I used to have very few memories of our childhood, and the memories I did have were unpleasant. When my sister spoke about our childhood, she always shared happy, joyful stories. I told her countless times, "I have no idea whose family you grew up in, but it wasn't mine." As I underwent my healing journey, I pulled out old family photo albums. When I looked at them with an investigative eye, I realized they were full of pictures of me as a child in which I was genuinely happy! The kind of happiness where your eyes light up and your smile is beaming equally as bright. Birthday parties, playing in the snow, spending time with family who had come to visit from other parts of the world.

As someone who had been accustomed to laser-focusing on my wounds, imagine the surprise I felt when I realized there were tons of pictures of me experiencing genuine happiness and joy!

Looking at those old family albums was an eye-opening experience. Until that point, I didn't have access to the positive experiences of my childhood. As it happens for many, the wounds of my childhood had clouded over the joys. I couldn't see beyond my hurt. All I could see and connect with were the stories of my pain and suffering.

The human mind likes to focus on the bad. From an evolutionary standpoint, the survival and preservation of our species was all that mattered. To survive, the species has to remember what danger looks like. Happiness and joy aren't helpful. Too much laugher won't kill you; a tiger will (unless, of course, you were attacked by a tiger in the midst of laugher, in which case, your mind will decide that laughter *is* dangerous and *will* kill you). The mind had no reason to imprint joyous memories.

The tricky little quirk about the brain is it doesn't know the difference between what's real and what's imagined. The brain doesn't know that the thought of a tiger isn't an actual tiger. We don't encounter tigers much in today's world. Instead, we take perceived threats to ourselves and turn them into tigers. We're constantly on the lookout for danger and wonder why we're feeling anxious.

As we move through healing and recovery, the absence of anxiety may lead us to feel more anxious, so we make things up to help us feel those familiar sensations of anxiety, chaos, and discord. We decide to get upset because someone is disrespecting us, when in reality, they're just too busy at the moment to give us their full attention. Sometimes, it's too distressing to let go of the anxiety. What will we do with ourselves in its absence?

Stress researchers tell us that humans can become addicted to adrenaline—the stress hormone. Adrenaline gives us a sense of aliveness that comes from the excitement of the stress. Don't believe me? Think about the last time you were running late. You knew you had to leave the house by a certain time to get to dinner on time. Still, you pushed through that one last thing you needed to do, just so you could finish it (because folding laundry is more important than dinner with friends, right?). When you looked at the clock, it was fifteen minutes later than when you wanted to leave. The panic sets in, your nervous system goes on high alert, and you perceive danger everywhere. You're feeling rushed, in a hurry, driving like a maniac, cussing at why other people can't drive, getting annoyed at every red light—and feeling the adrenaline pulsing through your body, giving you a sense of exhilaration and aliveness.

The rush you get when you add just a little bit of stress to your life gives you that small jolt of excitement, that jolt of adrenaline, that you mistake as the feeling of being alive. We have become addicted to stress, drama, and chaos as a way to get the adrenaline rush.

There's no better place to feel stress, drama, and chaos than in our interpersonal relationships. If you're anything like me or anyone I have ever worked with, you too have likely developed an addiction to stress. When your life is going smoothly, you don't know what to do with yourself in the absence of stress. You find opportunities to experience the adrenaline rush by creating stress, drama, and chaos within yourself.

As you start to become honest with yourself through the practice of fierce authenticity, you will start to notice how many of your day-to-day actions and relationship patterns are based on your addiction to adrenaline and your damaging need to have stress, drama, and chaos fuel your life.

Relational Mirrors

Back when I was creating chaos in my life and my relationships, I had no idea that what I was doing externally was actually a reflection of what was happening inside me. Even though I had an undergraduate degree in psychology and a master's in social work with an emphasis on clinical (counseling) services, I still had no awareness whatsoever about myself. I couldn't see that what I was putting out into the world about my relationships was my own inner turmoil, externalized. It took me *forever* to realize that everything that happens in my external reality reflected how I felt in my inner world. All of the people, places, and experiences in my life were simply a relational mirror showing me how I felt about myself.

At the age of 30, when my beautiful relationship with the man I knew I was meant to marry fell apart, I had the most painful, yet incredible, experience of my life: I had a spiritual awakening that finally put me on the path to seeing my own patterns in my relationships and how I had created every single one of them.

During that painful time of my life, I began to understand that our relationships are mirrors for us: everything we see in others is simply a reflection of ourselves. The people we attract into our lives are opportunities for us to see something about ourselves. With this awareness, we can make conscious and empowered choices.

When I first began my private psychotherapy practice, I thought I was going to work with single women to help them learn how to date. As it turned out, the women I kept attracting into my practice were married. They either wanted to bring their partners in for marriage therapy or to save their relationships by working on their own issues. They had already experienced too many relationship failures in their lives.

Amy is a good example of this. She wanted couples counseling. Her marriage of more than twenty years had been going sour for some time; she felt completely unsupported by her partner. According to her, the man who married her and vowed to keep her safe wasn't doing what he said he would. Her husband's lack of support left her in situations where she felt emotionally unsafe. She didn't know what to do.

In my first conversation with Amy, I explained that I do my best work with one person in the relationship. I told her that when one person does the work on themselves, the entire dynamic of a relationship has the potential to change. I offered Amy some referrals to couples' counselors and said that if she wanted to work with me individually, I would be happy to do so. We said our goodbyes—and within minutes, my phone rang again. It was Amy, calling back to say, "I want to make an appointment with you."

During our work together, Amy shared stories about her husband's lack of support, especially as it related to his mother. Amy came from a culture where mothers-in-law were seen as all-powerful beings who were to be respected no matter what. Any form of disagreement or standing up for herself would mean Amy was disrespecting her cultural and family values. As a woman of South Asian descent, I knew very well the traditions she was struggling with. It's a delicate line to walk. Thankfully, Amy wanted to feel better in her marriage and was willing to dive deep into her own inner work.

What Amy learned was that her mother-in-law reminded her of her own mother. The lack of support she felt from her husband was actually the lack of support she felt in her own ability to ask for what she needed in her marriage and in her life.

Because her mother-in-law reminded her so much of her own mother, it brought Amy back to feeling like a helpless little girl facing her own mother whenever her mother-in-law was mean or disrespectful to Amy. When she felt like that, any ability Amy may have had to ask for her needs flew out the window. She was too afraid to ask for what she needed. Instead, she had temper tantrums, as any five-year-old would—except she was doing them in her grown-up body. She would yell at her husband about what a terrible person his mother was and how it wasn't fair that he wouldn't speak up for her. This landed them into arguments that left her feeling more frustrated, unsupported, and alone than before, especially when her husband stormed off so he wouldn't have to hear her blaming and yelling.

Amy also realized that her mother-in-law triggered all of her own feelings of how not-enough she felt she was. Growing up with an overbearing mom who had rigorously high expectations of her, Amy was left feeling as though nothing she ever did was good enough. As the cosmos would have it, when Amy found and fell in love with her husband, she also fell into a family with a pattern very similar to her own.

Amy had unhealed wounds about her enoughness. Her mother-in-law seemed to know how to push every single one of her not-enough buttons: her housekeeping, her mothering, her ability to be a dutiful wife and caretaker. By doing the work, Amy realized that these were all areas where she herself felt not enough. She often questioned whether her housekeeping skills were up to par, whether she was a good cook, whether she was a good mother and a good wife. She suffered in silence, never allowing herself to let on to anyone how she felt inside.

When her mother-in-law pushed those not-enough buttons, they triggered her insecurities in these areas. When her husband didn't stand up for her, she saw more evidence of how not-enough she was … because if she was good enough, smart enough, attractive enough, he would stand up for her, right?

Viewing relationships as mirrors can be a total mind trip. You think someone is doing something *to* you, when they're really only showing you something you already feel about yourself. Looking at the ways you feel you are inadequate (even though you beat yourself up about it all the time) is uncomfortable. When someone triggers your feelings of not-enoughness, they now become the culprit and the object of your loathing and despair. Rather than look-ing inside yourself and examining your own stories, you make it about the other person and identify them as the villain in your story. You *dis*-own your own stories, your own thoughts, your own feelings, your own behaviors, and you make it about someone else. As you do this, you give greater power to the stories of your powerlessness and your wounding.

When you disown your inner stories and place them on somebody else as though *they* are the problem, you get to stay in a space of victimhood and disempowerment. You give away all your own power in the situation. The story remains, "See what a bad place the world is and how terri-ble people are? This is exactly why people can't be trusted and I'm not safe. This is exactly why I need to keep myself shielded and possibly even hidden from others."

By living your life in stories such as those, you keep yourself small, stuck, isolated, and alone. You don't allow yourself to be truly seen and heard for who you are. You perpetuate the stories of how not good enough you think you are.

On the flip side, the awesome news about your rela-tionships as mirrors is, if you allow yourself to know and *remember* that your relationships are simply reflections of how you feel about yourself, you can have access to a tremendous amount of growth and personal development in love and life. The opportunity for you to grow into the person you are truly meant to be, so you can experience the joys and the gifts life has to offer, is tremendously exciting. In addition, when you see desirable and admirable traits in another person, it means you possess those qualities and traits, too.

The Persian poet Rumi says, "If your mirror is not rubbed, how will it be polished?" It took me a long time to figure that one out. When it finally clicked, it became one of my favorite ways to view relationships: opportunities for my mirror to get polished, because boy, oh boy, rubbed wrong is the way I had felt most of my life.

The hurts and wounds you experience in your early relationships create the framework, or template, for the rest of your relationships to follow. The stress, drama, and chaos you invite into your life as a way to cope with your relational wounds fuel the stories of your not-enoughness. And lastly, relational mirrors are the opportunities you have to see yourself clearly and to heal.

Armed with this new information, I invite you to notice, what's arising for you as you contemplate your relational anatomy?

HEALING YOUR RELATIONSHIP WOUNDS

Your relationship patterns weren't born overnight. They're not going to heal overnight. The process of healing can be a long road, but it is also one of the most-rewarding roads you will ever travel. Healing your relationship wounds clears the path to more freedom, more success, and more fulfillment in all areas of your life. You will feel more at ease in your relationships, you will show up more authentically at work, and people will actually enjoy being around you on a whole new level. The exciting part is, the only person you have to depend upon for this process is you.

I have heard time and time again, "If only my husband, mother, boss, daughter, would change, then my life would be okay." The thing is, your husband, mother, boss, daughter aren't going to change because you want them to. The person who is going to change is you. Once you change, your perspective changes. Once your perspective has changed, you take on a whole new view of the world.

The things your husband once did that irked you won't irk you anymore. You'll start to view the fact that your mother is overbearing and tells you what to do as an endearing trait about her that stems from her own feelings of insecurity and her feelings of not-enoughness. Your boss won't overlook you for promotions anymore because you'll either allow yourself to show up and be seen and heard, or you'll decide it's time to move on to somewhere where you will be seen, heard, and respected. As for your daughter; well, you'll learn to love her exactly as she is, too.

You will begin to experience little life-changing miracles as you cultivate the practice of fierce authenticity in your life. When you are fiercely authentic with and for yourself, you can accept others exactly as they are. You will learn not only how to accept them, but also how to love them. Nobody wants to feel as if we don't love them and accept them exactly as they are. We all just want to love and be loved exactly as we are. An even greater gift? When you learn to love and accept others as they are, you start to love and accept yourself more fully, too.

The process of healing your relationship wounds is a simple one: You learn how to take care of yourself and relate with yourself from the position of unconditional love and acceptance. You learn to relate with yourself the way loving parents would relate with their child. And once you learn how to relate from a space of unconditional love and compassion for yourself, you then take this same love and compassion and radiate it out into the world, so all your interactions are infused with the same love and care you have for yourself. In a world that seems to run on fear, we need a whole lot more of us operating from love, kindness, and compassion. What we give out, we get. Rather than putting out fear, let's put out love.

The way to heal relationship wounds is what is known in psychological circles as re-parenting work: you learn to parent yourself and give yourself what you felt was missing from your childhood. This means you need to get in touch with your inner little girl who has felt hurt inside—the inner little girl who has been protecting herself for a long time. You need to connect with the child inside who has learned adaptive ways to navigate the world around her. By doing so, your little girl inside can learn the world is a safe place with the functional, grown-up you at the helm.

And don't worry about re-parenting. Unlike what some others teach about re-parenting, I won't make you walk around in a onesie with a blanket, a binkie, and a teddy bear ... unless you want to.

A WORD ON BLAME

Part of the healing work is to feel what arises and allow yourself to move through it. Sometimes what arises is the feeling of blame. As you contemplate the information and suggestions in this book, you might find yourself wanting to blame others for the way your life has turned out. Great! Feel the blame, feel the anger, feel the sadness, feel the disappointment, and feel every other feeling that arises within you. Then, once the feelings have moved through you, come back to these truths: Every relationship and interaction we have is an opportunity to heal. In any given moment, we have the opportunity to choose differently.

What once plagued you and kept you in the story of your wound can become your greatest gift, *if* you allow yourself to move through the process. Once you have discovered your own personal greatest gift, you can then choose how you wish to live your life. As Carl Jung said, "Until you make the unconscious conscious, it will direct your life and you will call it fate." Until you know the patterns and stories that have been running behind the scenes of your life, you will continue to play out the same old reruns as your reality. Once you know what your script has been, you can choose to do things differently. You can write a new script.

In the meantime, it is important to feel each and every feeling that arises for you. Part of the process of healing is the process of detoxification. When you experienced your wound, created a story about yourself and your worthiness (or lack thereof), and began to operate in the world by shielding your wound, protecting it, and keeping it safe from further harm, you also stopped the feeling process.

Emotions are simply energy in motion. When you

don't allow your emotions to move, they get stuck. Stuck emotions become toxic and lead you to shut parts of yourself off. When you make the decision to heal, you agree to allow yourself to go through a detox of all of the thoughts and emotions you weren't allowed to feel that had gotten stuck and stagnant inside you.

Detox often looks like lots of crying and experiencing feelings you stopped allowing yourself to feel. Tears are just frozen feelings thawing out, so when you start to notice yourself feeling uncomfortable and water begins to gush out of your eyes, know that you are simply in the process of thawing out what was once frozen. Staying present with yourself for this process is crucial.

When you jump straight from awareness of a pattern or a feeling to attempting to change it or accept it too quickly, you're bypassing the feeling and the detoxification. When you bypass the process, you're only prolonging your pain. This is why support is crucial to the process. If the process becomes too difficult, pull out your list of support people and reach out to them. It may not make the process any less painful, but this will make it more bearable. As you reach out to your support people, you'll learn that when you allow yourself to be witnessed through your process and see that others don't run away from you in fright, you'll start to gather more evidence of your inherent worthiness. It's a beautiful experience, and it's also the first steps toward allowing yourself to show up, be seen, and get love. ♥

Now that you have become familiar with relational wounds, where they came from, and how they operate in your life, you are ready to move into the four foundational principles of the practice of fierce authenticity. In the next chapter, we dive headfirst into fierce love (for yourself). You'll learn about the misconceptions around loving yourself, what loving yourself really means, and how you can cultivate deeper love and intimacy with yourself as a basis of cultivating deeper love and intimacy with others.

2

FIERCE LOVE
(for Yourself)

You owe yourself the love
you so freely give others.
—Unknown

'm sure you've heard it a million times: "You have to love yourself." Usually people fall into two camps when they hear this phrase: those who roll their eyes at it, and those who smile and nod in agreement, while on the inside asking, "What the earth does that even mean?"

Loving ourselves has become one of those buzz phrases people throw around, especially in the self-help and personal development industries. People often mistake loving themselves for doing things like going to yoga classes and getting mani-pedis, but loving yourself means more than just manicures. And quite frankly, yoga classes and manicures are better-suited for our conversation around fierce care of yourself, which we will explore in the next chapter.

What I am going to share with you in this chapter is about how you can create a definition of loving yourself in a deeply fierce way. Loving yourself in a way that allows you to suit up, show up, and love all of yourself, no matter what; a way in which you can love yourself when life is easy and even when it's hard. I'm going to help you create a definition of loving yourself that's so powerful, you will be able to change the world, simply by the way you show up for yourself.

When I speak about loving yourself in a fierce manner, I mean truly, deeply, loving yourself, as though you would love a child: with pure, innocent, gentle love and kindness.

The problem most of us have is that we don't treat ourselves with gentle love and kindness. Most of us are usually telling ourselves stories of how badly we suck and how much we can't get it together, why we don't deserve good things or experiences ... then we take all of that and beat up on ourselves. It's a vicious, never-ending cycle. It's one of those trips down the rabbit hole where one moment you're looking and feeling pretty good with yourself, then *wham*, something happens; hits you as though it came out of left field; and before you know it, you are in a deep, dark hole, filled with misery and despair. I know it well. For a long time, I used to live my entire life this way. So did Annette.

Annette, like most of my clients, was a master of disguise: she put on a persona of being well-mannered, well-adjusted, and well-put together. She was a mid-level executive in her company and did her job exceptionally well. Her co-workers and employees liked her, she did great work, her team functioned like a well-oiled machine … yet, when it came to her inner world, Annette was a mess.

"I don't think this is the right job for me. I am terrible at it, I can't seem to get anything right," she would say to me in frustration as she sat across from me on the couch, fighting back tears in her eyes. "I didn't even want to do this job, I didn't even want to study this stupid subject, and now I feel like it's the only thing I have. What am I supposed to do?"

Annette was falling apart inside.

Annette felt she was pressured into finance because that's what her family wanted her to do. She came from a family who prided themselves on advanced degrees, and since she was good at numbers, her family believed she should study finance. Yet Annette hated finance. She could acknowledge it paid her bills, gave her a beautiful home, and allowed her to eat out regularly. In our private sessions, though, she could also acknowledge it wasn't the thing that lit her up inside. Annette was doing it because she thought she was supposed to; because that's what was expected of her.

When we started diving into Annette's history, we learned she felt her parents only showed her love and affection if she did exactly what they wanted her to do, including excelling academically. Annette learned early on that the way to get any positive attention from her family was to get those straight As and do exactly as they said. Otherwise, they withheld their love and gave her the cold shoulder. Oftentimes, they would actually tell her she wasn't good enough.

During our work together, Annette realized that, as a grown woman, she did these very same things with herself. If something didn't go exactly the way she wanted it to go, or perceived it should go, Annette would begin to withhold love from herself and start to treat herself with a barrage of negative comments about how badly she sucked. In the absence of her parents, Annette became the one telling herself she wasn't good enough.

The moment Annette realized this was the pattern in her life, tears began streaming down her face, "Oh, my gosh, that is *exactly* what I do! It's like my parents live inside my head, even though they aren't even here!"

Bingo! That's when the magic of transformation began on Annette's journey to fiercely loving herself.

As I mentioned in the previous chapter, most of us had experiences as children that led us to feel less lovable. Whether it was your mom not standing up for you when the neighborhood kids were picking on you or your dad being at work all the time, all of us have a story about our unlovability. When we are in the story of our unlovability, we fall into the trap of withholding love from our selves. We become our own worst enemies. We become mean and cruel to ourselves. We withhold our own love from ourselves. And we keep ourselves stuck in vicious, never-ending cycles of pain. This chapter will help you recognize when you are entering into those cycles of pain.

THE INSTA-WALL

We communicate with ourselves and others through story. Stories are the thread weaving together the fabric of our being, of our society, of our civilizations. Stories tell us between right and wrong, they tell us how to behave, they tell us what our history is, and what happens when we follow— or don't follow—the path of historical data. Remember: Research tells us the mind makes meaning through stories.

The stories we tell ourselves are an important part of

my teaching. Stories are powerful because of the *feelings* they invoke in us. Stories aren't necessarily about the words; they are about the experiences and the feelings. When you hear a story that sticks with you, it probably sticks with you because of the feeling it invokes in you. You may not remember the words, but you remember how you felt.

The stories you tell yourself operate in the same way. These stories are based in the feelings you feel within your body. Our bodies are powerful storytellers. They carry the wisdom of our entire lives in them. Researchers have demonstrated that our memories, and our stories, live in our bodies. The body also tells us stories of our not-enoughness or our unlovability.

When you fall into stories of your not-enoughness and your unlovability, which really are one and the same, you fall into a pattern of closing yourself off, restricting yourself, or cutting yourself off from others. I refer to this as the "insta-wall": the wall that goes up immediately the instant we feel the story of our not-enoughness or unlovability coming up. What makes the insta-wall so dangerous is that most of the time, it is an automatic process that only takes a split-second to activate. Most of the time, you don't have any awareness that you are living and operating behind a wall.

I used to live behind these walls all the time, even as

I was working on healing them. Initially, I had no aware-ness that these walls even existed. I simply knew I was filled with judgment and all sorts of reasons why someone else wasn't worthy of connecting with. Thankfully, as I began to walk through my own journey toward fierce authenticity, I began to recognize a few things:

1. That there was a wall,
2. When the wall went up, and
3. What stories led to building the insta-wall in the first place.

As I walk my clients through the process of fierce authen-ticity, they begin to learn and recognize the same.

Perla is a woman I had been working with in my prac-tice for a couple of years. She had a great career as a C-level executive in her fast-growing and highly impactful compa-ny; she was often in the public eye; and her work was scru-tinized by the masses—it was impeccable, and 99.9 percent of the time, there was nothing negative anyone could say about her. Her inner perfectionist and hustler made sure of it, and she regularly received the highest of accolades. Yet, she struggled with stories of her enoughness. Perla had stories constantly running through her head that she was either "not enough" or "too much."

This belief of "not enough/too much" is a common

phenomenon I have noticed in the stories of the people I have worked with, women and men alike. Women are often taught we're too much or not enough. "You're too much like a boy. You're not enough like a girl." "You're too nice." "You're not assertive enough." Men are taught, "You're too soft. You're not man enough." "You're too hard." "You're too sensitive." "You work too much, you're never home enough." The list goes on and on for both genders.

These are the stories society tells us, which then become the stories we tell ourselves. We have to be "just right" to get love and affection. We are conditioned to believe that to receive love and affection, we have to be exactly a certain way. This is the conditioning that has to be unlearned, or *de*-conditioned, if you're going to make significant shifts in your beliefs about your lovability.

Perla had been making significant progress in recognizing where the stories of her not-enoughness were operating in her life, especially as they related to work. We had shifted to looking at where her beliefs of her not-enoughness were operating in other areas of her life, such as friendships and romantic relationships. One day, during a deep and intense session, Perla looked at me with fire in her eyes. Her nostrils flared as she said, "I can't believe he said that! I want to tell him to just pack up his shit and move out!"

Based on the way Perla was reacting, you would have

thought her partner had done something terrible. In reality, she was recounting a story in which her partner was sharing his cynicism about relationships. According to what Perla was saying, her partner had made no direct mention of her or their relationship. He was simply sharing his current thoughts about relationships in general.

"Perla, I'm reminded of that wall you've been working so hard to take down. It almost sounds to me like, in just a quick instant, your wall immediately went back up and you were trying to shut him out," I gently said to her in response. "It's like an insta-wall: The bricks you've been working so hard to take down, piece by piece, during the course of our work together all went back up into a fully reconstructed wall in an instant."

Silence.

Then, with newfound awareness, Perla responded, "Yes, that's what happened. I was scared the opinions he was sharing about relationships meant he felt that way about our relationship, too. Rather than experience the pain of getting hurt again, I wanted to push him out."

In that moment, Perla was able to recognize that the stories of her not-enoughness and her unlovability were at play. Thankfully, by that point in our work together, she had already realized that when she begins to feel vulnerable, she immediately defaults back to the old behavior of keeping others out while trying to keep herself safe within the walls she builds around herself.

This is what your stories do. They keep others out and they keep you small, stuck, isolated, and alone behind your insta-wall. You think your walls keep you safe from the perceived danger of opening yourself up to love. Whenever a story is triggered or activated within you, you shift into the default or automatic behavior of self-preservation: You attempt to keep yourself safe by keeping others out. What you don't realize is that in taking down those walls, you're able to achieve a true sense of peace, love, joy, and fulfillment in your life.

The amount of love we are able to receive is equal to the amount of love we have for ourselves. As a wonderful text called *A Course in Miracles* tells us, we can only receive at the level at which we are open to receiving. In much the same way that debris obstructs the flow of a river, you can only receive as much love as there is a clear path to you. That's what makes fierce love for yourself the first part of the practice of fierce authenticity. You need to clear out the debris that is obstructing the flow of love into your life.

WHAT STORIES DO YOU TELL YOURSELF?

Your stories play a crucial role in how you perceive yourself and how you treat yourself as a result. Your stories are the unconscious beliefs you have about yourself—you don't even know you have them. As long as the stories remain hidden in your unconscious, they will continue to run your life and you will think life is unfair. It will feel like life is happening *to* you. When you believe life is happening *to* you, all of your power lies outside yourself, rather than inside you, where it rightfully belongs.

With the belief that life is happening *to* you, powerlessness and hopelessness have room to enter your life and lead to a sense of despair. My whole purpose for writing this book is to help you shift out of despair and into empowered wholeness. That's part of what living a fiercely authentic life is all about.

If you're up for the challenge of developing awareness of your personal stories, starting today, pay attention to your thoughts and what you felt in your body when you had each thought. I suggest doing this check-in five times a day. As you pay attention to your thoughts and bodily sensations, ask yourself: What triggered your negative thoughts and beliefs about yourself? What stories were you telling yourself? What did it feel like in your body? How did your day/your mood/your perspective shift every time you found yourself in these thought patterns?

There are no right or wrong answers, only awareness as you cultivate the practice of fierce love for yourself.

LOVING *ALL* OF YOU

Back when I used to live in the stories of how not-enough I thought I was, my not-enoughness was all I could focus on. Just like Perla, on the outside I looked really good, but on the inside, I was constantly questioning who I was, what I was doing, and looking for evidence of all of my wrongs. The evidence of all of my wrongs, were of course, the ways I was either not enough or too much.

As I began deepening into my own healing work, all of a sudden, I began noticing moments in which the old stories would arise. Rather than allowing them to take me down into despair, I began to question them instead. "Is it really true that I totally fucked that up and therefore I suck? Or is it possible that my lack of grace in that interaction was because I'm learning a new skill set for relating?" Once I started questioning the stories I had initially learned about myself, a whole new life opened up to me: one where I got to start loving *all* the authentic parts of me.

The stories you tell yourself are incredibly powerful. Their power can be harnessed for constructive purposes or for destructive ones. The stories you tell yourself can be about how not-enough you are, or how much you suck, or how unlovable you are. Or the stories you tell yourself can be about how amazing you are, how loved you are, and how perfectly enough you are.

For now, let's learn more about the destructive nature of stories. When you tell yourself stories about your not-enoughness, your unlovability, or how much you suck, you begin a pattern of exiling certain aspects of yourself out of your conscious awareness. This is the very reason unchecked stories are dangerous. When you have stories and beliefs that you are "too much," you might attempt to turn off those "too much" aspects of yourself. As a result of turning off these parts of yourself, you create parts of yourself that you have disowned and exiled into the shadows of your psyche.

What lives untended in the shadows of your psyche can appear at the most inopportune times and say or do the most inappropriate things. It's similar to those times when you're having a great day, then something happens, and before you know it, you're having a fit and end up saying things you aren't proud of saying. It's usually the things you aren't proud of saying that come from the shadows of your psyche where your disowned parts reside.

Working with the shadow parts of the psyche is a complex subject, and the topic of numerous scholarly works.

To simplify it for our purposes, Kayla's story helps. Kayla called me one day, saying her marriage was in shambles and she needed help. In a tone of frustration, Kayla was able to communicate that she felt her mother-in-law hated her, her wife didn't care, and her friends were the only salvation she felt she had—but she was starting to treat them in ways she wasn't too happy about. Kayla told me she had been isolating herself and turning into an island. She was afraid that if she didn't get help right away, she might succeed at pushing all of her friends away.

Kayla and I began to work together to help her better understand the underlying patterns at play in her relationships.

"I don't know what's going on," she said during one of our sessions. "I've been getting more and more snappy with my friends, and they've started to distance themselves from me. I invite them to connect and they say they're busy. They tell me they don't have time, and then I hear they have been meeting up for coffee and dinner without me. What the hell? I don't understand!"

When I asked her what was different about herself, she paused and said, "Well, I *have* been more irritable lately."

"What happens when you get irritable?" I asked her.

"I kind of lose control of my tongue," Kayla said, and then paused. "I have a way with my words: I'm sharp-witted, but I can use my tongue for really mean and cutting comments as well. I think I might have started to get snappier with them … and I might have started saying some unkind things." Another pause, "Yeah, actually I did. I did say some pretty hurtful things. They would call me out on it; they would tell me my comments hurt. And then I would say more mean things back about how they just need to grow up. Sometimes I can't help myself. I don't know what comes over me."

When Kayla said "Sometimes I can't help myself, I don't know what comes over me," was the exact moment I knew Kayla was operating from a story based on a part of her that had been shunned out of her conscious awareness and shoved deep into the shadows of her psyche.

As we explored it further, Kayla recalled when she was a young girl, she was always quick-witted and good humored.

"I was really funny. I had comebacks for everything, and I always made my siblings and friends laugh. It got me into a lot of trouble, though. When I was young, although my quick wit and humor won over my siblings and friends, my parents and my very old-school grandparents used to tell me it's not 'ladylike' to be quick-witted. They'd say, 'Girls are meant to be seen and not heard.' They even said, 'Jokes are for the poor.'"

As a young girl, Kayla interpreted these messages to mean that her humor, her quick- wittedness, and her verbal expression of herself were parts of her that were unwelcome and therefore not okay. Based on her family's messages, Kayla believed she wasn't allowed to have or express those traits, so she did what most children do: She tucked them safely into a little box and put them away, exiling these parts of herself into the dark inner reaches of her mind, disowning them, and denying herself permission to have access to them.

Whether you safely tuck these unwelcomed parts of yourself into the dark corners of your mind or forcefully exile them there, these parts of you are constantly waiting to be expressed. And they will. What you hide in the shadows won't simply go away. These parts will stay there, getting more and more hungry, waiting for their opportunity to strike. When they do, you find yourself engaging in a behavior that is uncharacteristic of you, and then saying, "Whoa, I don't even know where that came from!"

BONUS: INTO THE SHADOWS

Fiercely loving yourself means loving *all* of yourself, including the dark, shadowy parts. When you allow yourself to love these parts and integrate them as part of your whole person, they no longer have a reason to hide out and run the show from the background. Counter-intuitively, when you allow yourself to love and accept all of you, even these parts you aren't proud of, these parts start to feel your love and acceptance. They no longer feel the need to get your attention and express themselves in uncharacteristic, shadowy ways.

I would love for you to dive into the shadows and meet your parts. I have a super-special bonus healing meditation you can use to help you meet some of these long-lost and forgotten parts of yourself. You can download it over at www.fierceauthenticity.com. In this bonus meditation, I will guide you through an exercise of meeting some of the unconscious parts of yourself that are asking for your love and attention.

SHOWING UP FOR YOURSELF

In any given moment, when faced with any situation, you have the choice to show up for yourself or to abandon yourself. When you're practicing fierce love for yourself, you show up for yourself, no matter what. When you are in the stories of your unlovability, your stories lead you to abandon yourself. You cross your own boundaries, you violate yourself, and you fall out of alignment with who you truly, authentically are. When you abandon yourself, you reinforce the stories of how unlovable you think you are.

It's in abandoning yourself that you also push parts of yourself deeper into the shadows, further isolating parts of yourself from your conscious experience.

My client Natasha was a successful neurologist, yet her successes didn't translate very well into her romantic life. Time and time again, she felt the pain of her romantic interests leaving her. When Natasha and I began our work together, the story she came in with was, "Any potential suitors disappear, so there must be something wrong with me."

When we dug into Natasha's relationship behaviors, it became clear why her romantic interests disappeared.

"Shirani, I don't get it," she said. "All the guys I've ever dated are always super into me for a couple of months, and then, when I start to let my guard down and get close to them, they totally disappear. No return calls, no texts, nothing. It sucks. I'm not sure what happens."

"Natasha, you present yourself as a highly confident woman, which you are—in most areas of your life. I imagine that's what most of your romantic interests are attracted to. That said, I also wonder, is there a switch that happens at some point? Do you step out of being your strong, independent, confident self, and step into being someone else?"

She thought about it for a moment, then quietly said, "Well, when I get really into a guy, I kind of stop focusing on myself and start to focus solely on him."

"And then what happens?" I asked.

"Then I start to act needy and want to hang out with him all the time. I stop making plans with friends or tell friends I can't plan with them because I need to see what he and I are going to be doing first."

"Uh-huh, and then what?"

"And then I start to call and text all the time and I freak out when he doesn't text me back within a few minutes, and then I get all freaked out and think he's going to run away."

"And then?"

"And then he runs away."

From there, we were able to get into Natasha's stories of her unlovability and why she began operating in ways that led her to abandon herself. Rather than showing up for herself, she gave up time with friends, then sat around the house upset when plans with her man never materialized. Natasha started bending over backward to spend time with him, whoever "him" was, even if that meant going over to his house to spend the night when she was exhausted and wanted to stay home for the night.

When Natasha got into stories of her unlovability, she

shifted into a version of herself who abandoned her own needs and desires for any crumb of attention her partners would give her. And for men, neediness isn't sexy. They would eventually either fall off the face of the planet or call it off with her.

Natasha abandoned herself. Maybe you do the same thing. You abandon yourself when you say yes to things when you would rather say no, when you do things you said you wouldn't, and when you outright withhold your own love and attention from yourself. This is why it's important for you to cultivate a fierce love for yourself—a love where you suit up and show up for yourself, no matter what. When you don't have love for yourself, it's going to be difficult for you to give or receive love. When you don't show up for yourself, nobody else can.

Your capacity to receive love is based on how much love you have for yourself. The same is true for how much love you are able to give. You can only love others as much as you love yourself. When you abandon yourself, neglect your needs, or violate and cross your own boundaries, you're reinforcing stories of your not-enoughness and your unlovability. When you make the decision to suit up and show up for yourself no matter what the outcome, even if that means disappointing someone else or letting another person down, or even if that means not seeing the person you're dating because you need some sleep, you're creating a new story about yourself: You're creating a story of how incredibly lovable you actually are. You're demonstrating a fierce love for yourself.

Through fierce love for yourself, your ability to give and receive love with others grows equally fiercely.

ENOUGH OR NOT ENOUGH?
THE CHOICE IS YOURS

Research shows that nine out of every ten thoughts we think about ourselves is a negative belief, one in which we are focused on our not-enoughness, our unlovability, and our flaws. That means in nine out of every ten thoughts that you think about yourself, you are affirming stories of how not-enough you are and how much you suck. Stories of your not-enoughness and your unlovability only keep love out. Wouldn't it be great if you could rewire your brain to believe in your inherent worthiness and just how lovable you are in nine out of those ten thoughts?

My invitation to you is simple: Every day, list at least three qualities or characteristics that you value about your-self. If you have a hard time coming up with qualities or characteristics of your own, think of things your friends, family members, and coworkers have said to you. Do they say you are funny, loving, and kind? Note those. Do they say you are perseverant, hardworking, and have a beautiful smile? Note those. No matter what they are, make a daily practice of listing at least three things you value about yourself each day. And don't worry if you can't think of anything new; you're allowed to repeat the same ones.

Keep on doing this as often as you can until your heart is able to feel the truth of the words you have been writing; until these thoughts become the nine out of ten you think about yourself a majority of the time.

Although this practice is a simple one, it's also powerful. Remember to keep showing up for yourself. By doing so over and over, you will build the muscle required to show up with fierce love for yourself.

Loving yourself seems like a simple task. It is, once you clear the blocks and the barriers that have gotten in the way of love's entry into your life. When your modus operandi is the stories that reinforce your not-enoughness and your unlovability, allowing love to enter into your life is a difficult task. When you make the decision to learn what your stories are, to meet the parts of you that have been shunned and are hiding in the shadows, and to stay true to yourself no matter what, the magic of loving transformation happens. Discovering what stories trigger your insta-wall and clearing the debris from the river of love that flows through your life allows you to start creating new stories about yourself: stories about how lovable you actually are.

Once you begin to practice fierce love for yourself no matter what happens, it only gets better. In the next chapter, you'll learn how fierce love for yourself leads to fierce care of yourself, much the same way a mama bear's fierce love for her cubs leads to fiercely caring for them. You'll also learn more about showing up for yourself and how that translates into experiencing greater love in your life. ♥

3

FIERCE CARE
(of Yourself)

When the well is dry, we know the worth of water.
– Benjamin Franklin

Women who attend my workshops and work with me individually share the same lament: "Shirani, I *do* take care of myself. I go to yoga, I make sure I eat well, I get manicures and massages. I don't understand. Why does my life still feel so empty?"

When we take that one step further, these women's actual question is, "Why do *I* feel so empty?"

The answer is simple: Fierce love for yourself lays the foundation for you to begin taking fierce care of yourself.

Most people think the two are interchangeable. In

my experience, they are two separate concepts that build upon one another. When you have deep and fierce love for yourself, you can take care of yourself on a whole new level: a level in which you engage in fierce care of yourself. Otherwise, you are simply engaging in surface-level acts of self-care, like taking yoga classes and getting manicures-pedicures, and wondering why you still feel empty inside.

To take fierce care of yourself, familiarize yourself with your stories, their origins, who your different parts are, and what your parts need from you to feel safe and secure. If you don't have love for yourself, it will be difficult to get into relationship with your stories, your parts, and your needs. It will be difficult to take care of yourself in ways that are meaningful and nourishing to you. That's why you'll keep doing the yoga, getting the massages, and continuing to feel empty inside.

A majority of the workshops I teach are attended by women, but men sometimes participate as well. Female or male, every single person in the room feels the same way about taking care of themselves—they were all taught it was selfish to do so! I was surprised to learn that even the men in the audience had received these same messages. Women have been taught this since the beginning of time. Women by nature are the nurturers, the caretakers, the ones who soothe the soul. Yet, we have a really hard time when it comes to taking care of ourselves or allowing ourselves to be taken care of.

Men have the same experience. As my work with men grew, it made sense. Men have been taught they are the providers, the ones who go out into the world and do what they need to do (even when they are things they don't want to do), to make money and put food on the table. They are taught their needs don't matter, they aren't supposed to have feelings, and they are expected to be providers without asking for anything in return.

When the men start to share this with us in workshops, it prompts quite the dialogue among the participants. Women start to realize they aren't the only ones who feel they're making sacrifices at their own expense. Most of the time, the women in the room had never thought of the struggle men face to take care of themselves.

As my work expanded to include couples counseling, this became more apparent. Men would say that when they come home after a long day of work, they feel pressure to be a partner or a dad. If they would rather relax alone for a bit first as a way to transition back to family life, they feel they're being judged. When women hear this, they often express feeling the same way.

It's a healing experience for men and women to share their stories and their struggles around caring for themselves and realize they aren't so different after all. When we can see our similarities rather than our differences, we learn to have a better understanding of one another. We develop an even-greater compassion for one another, and experience more love with and for one another. The story of "it's me *versus* you" becomes the story "it's about me *and* you." This is one of the most-healing moments the women and men I have worked with experience.

Regardless of gender, age, sexual orientation, or economic status, the stories we are taught are always the same: it's not okay to take care of ourselves; it's selfish to take care of ourselves; we need to always be there for others, sometimes at our own expense.

When you focus on fierce care of yourself, you can learn to show up and take care of yourself, while still being able to show up for others. Showing up for yourself while still being able to show up for others allows you to be seen and get love in a way that most people never imagine possible. When you learn it's okay to take care of yourself and that your relationships feel more satisfying and fulfilling as a result, you'll wish you knew this practice sooner.

Taking care of yourself first and foremost is the most selfless thing you can do for yourself and those around you. When you take care of yourself, you will always do what is most loving and kind for all involved. Why? Because you can't pour from an empty cup. Your own cup must be full to overflowing before you have anything to offer to another human being.

Filling your own reserve first makes you a more enjoyable person. Rather than giving from a place of depletion and possible martyrdom, you instead give from a place of love and joy. When you give from love, joy, and fulfillment, others feel that—and it helps them fill their cups, too. When you give from depletion, others can feel your resentment, and it leaves them feeling worse off than before. Now they feel they owe you something, or that they took something from you that you may not have had to give. Which way you choose to flow the cycle is up to you.

ANGER AND RESENTMENT

At the beginning of our time together, my client Sally often told me, "I am so frustrated. My kids asked me to take them to dance practice *again*! They knew I had to come here. They never ask my husband; they always ask me. Why does it always have to be me? Why can't they ask their dad? They always get in the way of me doing what I need to do. Just because I'm a stay-at-home mom doesn't mean I'm at their beck and call at all hours of the day. I have things to do, too!"

Sally loved her children, but with me, the resentment oozed out of her and she would sit on the couch seething in anger. She felt like a martyr and a victim, and it showed. In those moments, she seemed to have anything but love for her children and husband. Sally exuded so much anger and resentment that it was palpable not only in her words, but also on her face, in the way she held her body tight and tense, and in her overall energy field. Everything about Sally screamed, "I am so angry!"

Anger, resentment, martyrdom, and victimhood go hand in hand. Whenever someone asks "why" and pairs it with something that's happening to them, I know they're operating from a story. Take the question "Why does it always have to be me?" In this story, they are the victim and someone else is the villain.

I like anger. It's a powerful tool when harnessed well. Anger and resentment are powerful emotions that tell us we're out of alignment with our own best interests. When you can learn to use anger and resentment as tools for your healing, rather than as weapons to fling at others, you'll begin to make great strides in your practice of showing up, being seen, and getting love.

When you're as angry as Sally, it's obvious the anger isn't providing power. Kids are sponges and can sense with great accuracy what is going on in the people around them.

They also respond in kind to whatever the adults around them are emitting. I pointed this out to Sally, saying, "You know, Sally, I wonder how your kids respond to the anger and frustration that you feel about this?"

Sally paused. "What do you mean?"

"Well, most of the time, our children are really good at picking up what's going on with us. I wonder how your kids respond to your anger and frustration."

Sally thought for a moment. "Well, they tend to get more rambunctious when I'm feeling angry, which makes me feel even more angry and resentful. Then I get even snappier with them."

"And how do you feel when you get snappy with them?"

"Well, I guess I'm not really proud of myself in those moments. It actually feels really bad. I don't like yelling at them or getting snappy with them. It just happens. It's like I can't control it; it just flies out of my mouth. And then I feel bad about being short with them."

"And how do they respond?"

"They look at me like they're scared of me, kind of shrinking away from me, which feels fine in the moment because I don't want to be around them. But later, I feel bad knowing that because I got angry with them, they felt scared of me. I don't want them to feel scared of me. That's not what I want for my kids at all. I don't want it to be like when I was growing up."

Then, in that moment, she had a powerful awareness: "Ugh, I said I would never be my mother, and here I am, acting like my mother. Oh, no. What do I do?"

"You start to take care of yourself. You start to ask for help. You learn to say no, and you learn to redirect. That's what you do."

Sally's anger and resentment had its origin in her neglect of herself. A part of her was trying to get her attention and tell her she wasn't taking care of herself and her own needs.

TAKING FIERCE CARE OF YOURSELF

Like many of the women I work with, Anita constantly feels drained and exhausted by trying to meet all the demands her inner hustler says she has to meet. Her typical day actually begins the night before she awakens to start a new day. She's tired and ready for bed by 9:30 p.m., but she pushes herself past her limit, trying to do that one last thing. Before she knows it, it's 11 p.m. and she is beyond exhausted, but because she pushed herself too far, she's now restless and finds it difficult to fall asleep.

Anita wakes up in the morning grumpy, grumbling, and

cursing the day for arriving too soon. She feels as though she hasn't slept a wink. She drags herself out of bed, and before doing what she needs to do for herself, she instead groggily starts tending to her children's needs. She makes breakfast; checks that the kids are fed, their hair combed, and their teeth brushed; and gets them off to school, fueling herself with coffee. She leaves the house in a frantic rush, feeling like she is already behind for the day. When she gets to work, she does her best to be chipper. The reality, however, is she's tired and has a disgruntled inner dialogue all day long:

"Aaarrrgggh, my co-worker pisses me off! Why can't he just do his damn job?"

"Ohmigosh, that idiot didn't complete all of her work before passing it on to me. Why does she still work here?"

"Oh, man, I think I might have screwed up that email. I wasn't paying attention and my fingers hit Send too fast. Yup, they're gonna fire me now."

Sometimes her inner dialogue slips out as a snarky comment to one of her co-workers and she feels bad about herself.

Anita rarely takes a real lunch break. She snacks at her desk instead. She runs on coffee and chocolate all day, and doesn't move far from her desk. She often ends up working late as she tries to squeeze out one more email before leaving for the day. Then she races to pick up her kids, battling with road rage all the way. Once the kids are packed into the car, if she isn't already snapping at them, she makes a half-hearted attempt to be interested in what they have to say. By this point, though, she has very little bandwidth left for them.

When she gets home, she darts straight to the bathroom, realizing, "Oh, my gosh, I haven't peed all day!" And even then, she can't have any peace. The kids are fighting, pounding on her bathroom door. After yelling at them, she makes dinner in all-out zombie mode, takes them to whatever activities are on the schedule that day, and helps them with their homework. When she's finally ready to crash out, her husband attempts to initiate sex. Angrily she turns him down, annoyed that he would have the nerve after all she's done all day. Then finally, she passes out, only to rinse and repeat the next day.

Anita isn't the only woman whose day looks like this. She's not that different from many of the women I see. The one thing they all tell me is "I'm so tired!" paired with "There's never any time for *me*!"

What happened to Anita is she forgot how to be happy, she forgot how to be courageous, she forgot about herself. Anita had been programmed to believe that she needed to take care of everyone else so her world would not fall apart. Instead, she herself was falling apart.

As we began picking apart the thoughts behind Anita's frantic daily schedule, she realized she didn't believe herself to be worthy of self-care and asking for help. Her husband helped, but she didn't allow herself to ask him for more help and support. Anita had been taught a woman's role is to be Superwoman. She was taught it wasn't okay for her to take care of her own needs—she always had to put her husband and her children before herself. She wasn't allowed to ask for help, because she had bought into the idea that women are supposed to be able to do it all.

But Anita didn't feel or look like Superwoman. She felt like a haggard old lady. She looked older than she was, with dark circles under her eyes and skin that had lost its glow. She felt empty, hollow, and exhausted. She wasn't feeling satisfied or fulfilled in her life or her relationships at all.

Most of the women I have supported, whether in workshops, private sessions, or through mentorship, share the same story: "I feel like it's selfish to take care of me." I hear, "How will people react if I tell them I'm going to yoga tonight rather than helping with homework?" "My husband can't take care of dinner, he would burn it all." "My kids need to be carted back and forth to Tae Kwon Do, and there's no time for me." No matter what words they say, the story underneath is always the same: I am not worthy of taking care of me.

Taking care of yourself is really simple. It looks like taking care of your most-basic needs. It looks like making sure you are going to the bathroom when the need arises, and you are eating at regular intervals. It looks like moving your body, even if only for small stretch breaks throughout the day. It looks like putting yourself to bed on time, rather than trying to do that one last thing. It looks like asking your partner to step up and share more of the caretaking burden.

Practicing fierce care of yourself means you do whatever is necessary to protect and nurture your physical, mental, emotional, and spiritual health. You begin to practice fierce care of yourself simply by taking care of your most-basic needs first. When you feel tired, get some rest. When you feel hungry, nourish your body with real food. Drink ample amounts of water each day. Move.

THE RELATIONSHIPS-TO-NURTURE LIST

As you allow yourself to take better care of your most-basic needs, you will miraculously have more energy to help take care of everyone else's needs—with a smile on your face and joy in your heart. You'll be more present to the experiences around you. You'll be able to receive your loved ones when they approach you. Your thoughts will be clearer and the brain fog will lift. You'll experience clarity, presence, and joy at life's little moments, rather than missing them as they pass you by.

Modern women are taught to have a career, take care of others, and place themselves last on the relationships-to-nurture list (if they get a spot on the list at all). It's no wonder women have a hard time taking care of themselves! We try so hard to take care of others, but we do so without filling our reserves first. By placing yourself last on the list, you run the risk of approaching all of your relationships with an energy of depletion. When you're depleted, you have nothing to give others—your well is dry. That's when you perpetuate the exhaustion, frustration, and other feelings of not-enoughness.

To feel more peace, connection, flow, and ease in your life, I suggest you practice nurturing your relationships in this order:

Source

Self

Spouse

Children

Parents

All others

At the top of the list is Source. Allowing yourself to connect with a source of power greater than yourself, be that power a Source/Creator, God, the Divine, the Universe, or even just the oceans of the Earth, helps keep you connected to something bigger and greater than you that gives you direction for the day. You can connect with Source through journaling, prayer, meditation, or simply admiring the beauty of nature. By doing so, you can reduce your levels of anxiety and help restore yourself to levels of sanity that make you enjoyable to be around, resulting in more-loving relationships.

Taking care of yourself is the most selfless thing you can do. It allows love to flow more freely, it clears up feelings of anger and resentment, it frees you to give and receive in ways that feel good. Rather than using anger and resentment as weapons to fling at others, I invite you to take some time right now to get familiar with them as tools for your healing.

As you cultivate the practice of fierce care for yourself, it's helpful to list all the ways you take care of others' needs before you take care of your own. After you've taken some time to contemplate this, consider how you feel when you take care of others instead of yourself. Do you feel angry? Resentful? Do you feel tired? Do you feel depleted? Do you get "hangry," or irritable, or unreasonable? To balance the negative emotions, consider the positive. Do you feel fulfilled because taking care of others gives you a sense of purpose? Do you appreciate the love and thanks you get in return? Do others take care of you when you need it?

Finally, think about which way you want to feel. I know the answer for me, and for every single person I have ever supported, is I want to feel filled with love and positive energy.

A FIERCE *YES* TO YOU

Let's play a little game. When I say "boundaries," you notice what arises in you. Ready, set, go:

Boundaries

Pause. Breathe. Notice the initial reaction that arises from you. Don't question it; simply allow whatever the feeling is to arise.

Now again:

Boundaries

Pause. Breathe. Notice the next reaction that arises from you. Again, don't question it; simply allow whatever thoughts, feelings, words, or actions arise, to arise.

And one last time:

Boundaries

Pause. Breathe. Notice again what arises in you. Then,

allow yourself to take a few deep breaths, shake it off, and bring your awareness back to the present.

If you are like most people who struggle with showing up, being seen, and getting love, you might feel a slight sense of discomfort arise as you think about boundaries. Perhaps you feel a tightness in your chest, a feeling of constricted breathing, or maybe even a slight sense of nausea. You might feel your brain wander and begin to wonder, "What on earth are boundaries, really?" Discomfort with the idea of boundaries, or wondering what the word even means, are the two most-common reactions I get when I speak with people about boundaries.

Similar to the ideas of self-love and self-care, boundaries is a concept that's casually thrown around. Too often, we think boundaries are firm, rigid lines we draw to establish guidelines of how we believe others should be acting toward us. In reality, boundaries are firm yet flexible limits that we establish for ourselves. I like to think of a boundary as a permeable membrane. In the cells of your body, permeable membranes allow oxygen and nutrients to enter and wastes to leave, while keeping harmful toxins out. In our interactions with others, boundaries can play the same role.

Sometimes boundaries are physical separation, such as actual distance between you and another person. Other times, boundaries are mental and energetic separation—a sort of bubble that contains you within your space and keeps everyone else out. Boundaries can also be the written or spoken requests you have with other people (or even with yourself).

Boundaries are both delineations of where one area ends and another begins, and also limits that define behavior acceptable to us. Boundaries are the physical, mental, emotional, and energetic lines that delineate us as individuals separate from others.

The funny, and often frustrating, experience with boundaries is that others are always trying to find a way around them. How many times have you created a boundary, only to find that someone has pushed through it? You find yourself feeling angry and resentful all over again.

Boundaries are for you. They are for you to determine, establish, and enforce. Others will always attempt to find a way around your boundaries, especially if they want something from you. It's your job to enforce your boundaries.

Boundaries are the set of limits you establish for yourself to help make your own life more manageable. They are also the ways you communicate with others about what is and is not okay with you. When you haven't been taking care of yourself, and you have allowed yourself to fall into anger and resentment, you have either violated your own boundaries or might not have realized you needed a boundary in the first place.

Use your anger and resentment to guide you toward your own needs and set your own boundaries.

Most of the individuals I have supported who take care of others before taking care of themselves self-identify as "people pleasers." These are the people who would do anything for anyone else, at their own expense, just so they can be loved and accepted. The paradox is that people-pleasing rarely leads to love and acceptance. Instead, people-pleasing usually leads to greater anger and resentment, sometimes toward the very people you claim to love.

People-pleasing has its origins in your stories of not-enoughness. When you feel you are not-enough as you are, you don't set boundaries, or you let people violate them, in hopes they will love you.

Two concepts are very helpful for setting your boundaries. One is the simple idea of saying no. The other is remembering that when you stop pleasing people, people won't be pleased. When you implement these concepts, be prepared for pushback, from both your inner self and the people around you.

We don't allow ourselves to use the word "no" often enough. Women in particular think saying no is selfish and bitchy. I'm going to let you in on a little secret: Love says no. Sometimes the most-loving and kindest thing we can do is to tell another person no. When you say no, you allow yourself to honor yourself. A loving "No" to someone else is actually a loving "Yes" to you. You also allow the other person to find another way to get their needs met, giving them the dignity to figure it out for themselves. It's a win-win situation, although you may find it hard at first to put saying no into action.

My client Betty used to have a hard time saying no to people. She sat in session one day almost in tears and said, "Shirani, I did it again. I said yes when I wanted to say no, and now I don't have time for myself, I feel like I'm being a bad friend, and I keep flaking out on people."

"What happened?" I asked.

"My boss wanted me to take on another project, even though he knew I was already feeling overwhelmed, and of course, I smiled and said, 'Sure.' He knew I was already slammed and he still asked. He knows I'm that girl who can't say no. I am so mad at myself!"

"Betty, you mentioned flaking out, feeling like a bad friend."

"Yeah, because the other projects I already have are taking up so much of my time, and now that I said yes to this other really massive project, I don't have time for my friends. I keep flaking out on dinner; I forgot a really important birthday party; and when I do show up, I'm just a hot mess. Not present, tired, and really disgruntled about my job. I can't do this anymore! I seriously feel like I'm about to have a nervous breakdown or something."

That was the moment Betty recognized that she needed to make some major changes in her life. When we explored what was happening for her, it came down to the story of her not-enoughness. Like many of the people I have worked with, Betty thought she needed to do more, take on more, and hustle harder, just to show she was worthy of love, approval, and belonging.

I suggested to Betty that she start small. Practice by saying a loving no to requests and invitations from family and friends. She got to work on trusting that she is enough as she is, and recognizing how she violates herself by saying yes to things she doesn't have the bandwidth for, and her life started to turn around. As she started getting more comfortable with saying no to small requests and invitations with safe people, she allowed herself to start practicing with others, and eventually she was able to start saying no to her boss.

Betty realized that by saying no to others, she is actually saying yes to herself. By saying yes to herself, she was showing herself that she loves and accepts herself as she is—and that she loves herself enough to take care of herself.

As Betty realized, she is the only one who can take care of herself, and nobody can do it like she can.

After a few months of working on her new-found skill of saying no, Betty said in one of our sessions, "Shirani, I'm so excited! I feel like I have my life back! No—better: I feel like I now actually have a life! I can check in with myself when people ask me for things, I can decide if this is going to work for me or not work for me, and I can feel good saying 'No, that doesn't work for me.' And the best part is, when I say yes to me, I can show up better for others."

Betty had been transformed from the woman who was distraught at having said yes to things that didn't work for her. She was now a glowing woman, able to fiercely take care of her own needs before taking care of others.

ASK AND RECEIVE

Growing up, I was always told by the women in my family, "Grow up, get educated, stand on your own two feet, and then you can think about getting married." With messages such as that, it's no wonder I became a woman who was damned if she was going to let anyone else do anything for her. I was one of those strong, independent women who was going to do everything for herself. Women stereotypically can't read a map and can't navigate to save their lives?

Nope, not me. Women spend money willy-nilly and aren't able to manage their finances? Nope, not me. Women can't go out and buy cars on their own? Nope, not me. I was one of those warrior women who was going to do everything on her own, thank you very much.

Except it was an exhausting and lonely life. I wanted so badly not to have to do everything on my own. I was too prideful and had heard too many stories about how a woman was never supposed to rely on anyone, especially not a man. Like most of my clients, I was stressed out, burnt out, and at my wits' end. I knew that wasn't how I wanted to feel, yet I didn't know how to do things differently. It's what a friend of mine calls "the curse of the bright, educated, modern woman." On the one hand, we're raised to be super-independent super- achievers, and trained to do it all. On the other hand, the desire for love, connection, and a meaningful relationships is strong. In my relationships, I didn't know how to allow another person to be of service and help. I was perpetually stressed out, burnt out, and overwhelmed. I knew I wanted a different experience, but I didn't know how to let it in.

For me, and for most of the people I have supported, asking for help is terrifying. We're afraid of our stories of not-enoughness and afraid of being perceived as unable to do it on our own. The fear brings out our inner hustler and prevents us from even thinking of asking for help. That's why knowing our stories and where they come into play is a crucial component of fierce authenticity.

When you allow yourself to sit with and familiarize yourself with the stories of your not-enoughness, they stop having power over you. Once the stories have less power over you, you can start the loving actions you need to take to better care of yourself. One of those loving actions is taking fierce care of yourself. Part of taking care of you means asking others for help.

Not asking for help keeps you in the stories of your not-enoughness. It keeps you in the pattern of taking care of other people's needs at your own expense. Self-abandonment leads to believing you're not worthy of being taken care of—and the cycle repeats.

When we think of asking for help, we think that means we failed and couldn't do it on our own. The reality is, as humans, we are pack animals—social beings not meant to do things entirely on our own. In earlier times, we lived in tribes and villages, where everyone had a role and supported one another for the greater good. Modern society is more individualistic and isolated. We have lost the art of asking for and receiving help.

If asking for help feels like a difficult task, start small. Break it down into small steps. Go through the list of ways you take care of others' needs before your own. Look at each item and ask yourself, "Can someone else take care of this?" If the challenge is something only you can do, it's yours to handle. If the challenge is something that could be shared with or done by someone else, there's probably space for you to ask for help. Whom to ask? For household issues, your spouse or partner and the kids themselves. At work, your co-workers. At leisure, your friends. Also, don't be afraid to hire out for help.

Again, start small. If you have children, maybe it's time they started picking up after themselves. Does it have to be you who loads the dishwasher after dinner, or can your partner do that? If you're the one always putting out fires at work, are all of those fires yours to be putting out, or would it be best to step away and have the person who needs to put out that fire do it themselves? Can one of your friends organize the monthly girls' night instead of you?

As you start to ask others for help, keep it simple. Use words such as, "Can you please help me put the dishes away?" Or, "I need some help with the laundry. Can you please help?" Another suggestion: "I'm having a hard time getting to the grocery store. When would be a good time that you can help me?" In examples like these, you clearly state you need help and ask the other person to help you. When you ask, "When would be a good time you can help me?" you're inviting the other person to participate with you in a timeline that works for them. You aren't really asking them to help; you're saying you know they could help.

If it feels too uncomfortable to say these words out loud, begin by rehearsing the words in your mind. Allow yourself to get comfortable with them. The more you practice, the better you will become. If it feels awkward at first, that's okay. Not everyone who got on a bike the first time rode off into the sunset gracefully and with ease. Most people started with training wheels, and got a few bumps, scratches, and skinned knees along the way.

Remember Anita? Once she learned what she could ask for help with and began asking for it, she noticed resistance from her family. She said to me one day, "Shirani, you told me to start asking for help. We practiced it, and now my kids are pushing back with me. It's almost easier for me to do it myself and not ask them for help."

"Anita, any time you make changes to the way things have been, you're likely going to get some pushback. People don't like change, especially when the change isn't in their favor. You've been the 'do-it-all mom' for so long, doing things for others that they could do for themselves, that they don't see why they should start now. By asking for help, you're inviting them to step up and take responsibility—and do some work. People don't like that. I promise you, if you give in to them, they'll keep getting exactly what they want, and they'll lose a little bit of respect for you each time. They'll see you aren't going to stay true to your words and you aren't going to follow through with taking care of yourself. They'll deduce that if you aren't going to take care of you, they don't need to, either."

Anita was mind-blown. In all this time, she hadn't realized that when she goes back on her word, she loses the respect of the people around her, and her parts lose a little bit of respect and trust in her, too.

"No more. No more going back on my word. They are all just going to have to deal. I need to take care of me, and that's that." Anita was resolved to continue taking fierce care of herself.

Like Anita, you might find that when you finally ask for help and invite others to take responsibility for what is theirs, you'll experience some resistance and pushback, too. You too might find yourself wanting to go back on your word because it's easier than dealing with the opposition. Stay the course. Continue taking fierce care of you and asking for help. Eventually, when others see you're serious and you aren't going to violate yourself by going back on your word, they'll have more respect for you and will start to comply.

Often, when people resist change, they're really only

showing you where your own resistance lies. For Anita, her family's resistance was because she still wasn't so sure she was worthy of asking for help and allowing herself to receive it. To be effective at asking for help, you have to not only ask for help, you have to be open to receiving it, too.

Your ability to allow yourself to receive help is where the true magic happens. As you allow yourself to open up and ask for help, I want you to feel a sense of success. Just as your ability to receive love is based on how much love you have for yourself, the same is true of your ability to receive help. When you believe you are not worthy of receiving help and support, you will block any help and support that comes your way; or, the help you do receive will reinforce your stories of your not-enoughness.

Once Anita understood her blocks to receiving help, she was better able to ask for and accept it. Her children's objections no longer bothered her. Eventually, they stopped objecting and started complying. By the time Anita and I wrapped up our work together, she looked as though she had gotten years back into her life. Her face had a vibrant glow, she was no longer fueled by coffee, she stopped abandoning herself, she showed up fully for herself, and she was able to navigate through each day with a greater sense of peace and ease. This is what taking fierce care of yourself is about. What Anita experienced is my hope for you, too.

4

FIERCE AUTHENTICITY (The Goal of this Book)

It is in unbecoming that we become.

—Unknown

You begin to experience life-changing magic when you allow yourself to get intimately familiar with who you authentically are. By now, you've taken the time to get into a relationship with yourself based in fierce love and fierce care. You probably have begun to notice the little miracles that occur when you start to shift your perspective from fear to love and start to prioritize yourself—to put Source and yourself at the top of your list. You are likely to feel more energy, less depleted, and a whole lot less angry and resentful.

The practices of fierce love for yourself and fierce care of yourself have set you up beautifully to deepen into the practice of fierce authenticity.

Living your life with fierce authenticity allows you to feel more happiness, more joy, more love, more peace, and more ease in your life. When you tap into the practice of fierce authenticity, you experience more alignment and more flow—in yourself, your relationships, and the entire world around you. When you do that, you attract others into your life who are doing the same. Your life and your relationships will shift and be filled with more love and gratitude.

When you see a woman who sacrifices her authentic self in her longing to be loved, you realize that fierce love for yourself and fierce care of yourself form the core of the practice of fierce authenticity. Only after you learn to fiercely love and care for yourself will you stop seeking love and approval from the outside. Once you fully accept yourself for who you are, you can more easily recognize your own talents, gifts, and all the other beautiful aspects you bring to the table. Through the practices of fierce love for yourself and fierce care of yourself, you create room for authenticity to grow.

WHAT IS AUTHENTICITY, ANYWAY?

Authenticity means more than being real. It means being worthy of acceptance, not false or imitative. It means being true to your own self. It means living your life according to your own thoughts, feelings, desires, and needs.

Let's break authenticity down further. Something that is authentic is worthy of acceptance. You, as your authentic self, are worthy of acceptance. Something that is authentic is not false or an imitation. When you allow yourself to be authentic, you are not presenting yourself in a way that is false or imitative, based on what others want you to be. And lastly, when you are practicing fierce authenticity, you are true to your own personality, spirit, and character. Nobody else can be authentically you. Only you can do that.

When we put it all together, authenticity means you are worthy of acceptance, without presenting a false persona based on others. You are true to your own personality, spirit, and character.

To take it up a notch, fierce authenticity means you live from your true inner power. Your power resides in who you are at the core of your being, when you free yourself from the stories, the limitations, and the expectations you and others have placed on yourself. That means you determine who you are and what you want for yourself, based on your own inner guidance. You choose to live in and from your truth.

You know you're practicing fierce authenticity when you no longer look externally to define who you are. Instead, you look within and feel a strong and comfortable connection with your deepest self.

Fierce authenticity means you live in alignment with yourself.

KNOW WHO YOU ARE

You constantly receive messages from everyone around you—about who you should be, how you should act, what you should say, and what you should expect of yourself and others. Sometimes the messages are valuable and worth accepting. Sometimes they're confusing, unhelpful, undermining, and plain-out wrong. When you live with fierce authenticity, you know who you are and how to get beyond the messages that hurt you.

Meena began her work with me not knowing who she was. When I asked her what was her favorite food, what color she liked, what style of clothing she felt good in, she had no idea! She looked at me with a blank-faced stare.

"Shirani, I have no idea! I've never even thought about those things. I eat what my husband and my kids eat. Colors … I don't know. I mean, I always wear black and hadn't even thought of what colors I might actually like. Black is easy. It's just there, I don't have to think about it. And clothes? I wear whatever I find that fits. I actually haven't shopped for myself in ages!"

"In the past, how did you decide what you actually liked or didn't like?" I asked.

"I don't know. I guess I really only went with whatever other people liked." She thought about it for a moment and said, "Yeah, actually, I did go with whatever other people liked. In grade school, I liked pink because that's what all my friends liked. When I got to high school, I liked black because I was friends with all the goth kids. They liked heavy metal and grunge, so I liked heavy metal and grunge. They liked spiky collars, so I liked spiky collars. A teenage Indian girl wearing spiky collars—that was a sight to see. Actually, in looking back, I hated spiky collars and grunge music. But that was me, doing what everyone else was doing, hoping that it would get them to like me. It didn't get any better, either. In college, I joined a sorority—the total opposite from grunge days, I know—because the girls in my hall were joining a sorority. I didn't really care for it, but that's what they were doing, so rather than be left alone, that's what I did, too."

It was in those ten little words—"rather than being left

alone, that's what I did, too"—that the gifts of Meena's lessons lay.

"Meena, you say you didn't want to be left alone; that's why you went along with what others were doing. What might it have felt like if you knew back then that when you have a deeply intimate relationship with yourself, you're never alone?"

Meena was gob smacked. I could see it in her face. All thoughts came to a screeching halt and she said, "What if I were deeply intimate with myself? That sounds nice and all, but what does that even mean?"

I responded, "When we lose ourselves, or have no sense of who we are, it's easy to get caught up in what everyone else is thinking, doing, wearing, and so on. We want to fit in with the in-crowd, or at least we want to fit in with whichever crowd takes us in, so we simply go along with whatever they are up to, without even taking the time to get to know ourselves. Then, we feel empty and alone inside and wonder why life doesn't seem fulfilling."

"Yeah, empty and unfulfilling … that sounds about right," Meena quietly said.

"So, what do you think it might be like if you were to work on getting acquainted with yourself more deeply?"

"Wow, that would be amazing!"

And that's exactly what we did.

From there on out, my work with Meena was to help her get more deeply acquainted with herself, the way you would get acquainted with a lover or another VIP in your life. What did she like, what did she dislike, what was her favorite color or colors, what felt good to her, what didn't feel good to her, what style of clothing was her own, what music and movies did she enjoy? As we worked toward helping Meena get better-acquainted with herself, we also began to talk about how she could express her authentic self in the world.

Developing fierce love for yourself and fierce care of yourself lays the foundation for you to cultivate a deeply intimate relationship with yourself. When you fiercely show up for yourself with love and care, in the same way you show up for someone who is important to you, you are telling yourself that you are important and you matter. As you move forward in your relationship with yourself, as with any intimate relationship, you need to start learning more about who you are underneath it all. Without the base layers of fierce love for yourself and fierce care of yourself, getting to know who you authentically are is nearly impossible. If you've already begun to show yourself that you are an important human being and that you are worthy of your own love and attention, fierce authenticity is easier to achieve.

BE IN FIERCE INTEGRITY WITH YOURSELF

Getting better acquainted with yourself matters. If you don't know who you are, you'll have a difficult time being in integrity with yourself. When you make the decision to live in integrity with yourself, your whole world changes. Rather than relying on outside sources to validate you, your thoughts, your feelings, your opinions, and your actions, you instead choose to do what is right for you—even when others don't or won't agree. When you deny your integrity and ignore your better instincts, things can go sour.

One definition of integrity is being honest and having strong moral principles. When you have integrity, you act in ways that are consistent with the values, beliefs, and moral principles you hold. Integrity also means being open, honest, and responsible for all of your actions—and acknowledging and admitting when you've made a mistake.

In the practice of fierce authenticity, being in integrity means being true to yourself through your thoughts, behaviors, and actions. Being in integrity means your words and your actions match. You experience fierce integrity when you take the time to get quiet with yourself and reconcile what doing the right thing for yourself looks and feels like.

No one can tell you what being in integrity looks like

for you. Only you can determine it for yourself. The practice of fierce authenticity can help you live your life in alignment with your integrity. Being in integrity with yourself can be as simple as letting the cashier know when they've accidentally given you back too much change, or as complex as sharing what's on your heart, even when it might be off-putting to others. It means living and speaking your truth, even when your truth might be an unpopular one, or even when you're afraid you might lose a relationship because of it.

Experiencing anxiety is a sign that you're likely living out of integrity with yourself. Anxiety is your soul's signal that you're trying to please others at your own expense—whether those others are your parents, your partner, your children, your teacher, your boss, or your friends. Anxiety indicates that you're afraid to share your truth with those you want to please or impress. You fear that if you do, they will see your not-enoughness.

Sonia used to experience the anxiety of living out of alignment with who she is every single day, especially in her romantic relationship.

"Shirani, my partner wants more sex than I do and even though I don't enjoy it, I keep giving in to him," she said to me one day.

"Can you tell me more?"

"Sometimes I'm just not in the mood, and he insists we have sex," Sonia sighed, "so rather than feel like a bad girlfriend, I give in to him."

"Oh, okay." I acknowledged what she shared, then gently asked her, "How does that work out for you?"

"I go through the motions and fake the orgasm, all the while feeling terrible about it."

The sense of shame in Sonia's face was visible now. She knew that she wasn't living in integrity with herself. She knew she was violating herself.

"Have you been able to speak with him about this?"

"Well, I brought it up once before, and he kind of brushed me off. Told me to just lighten up and enjoy it. After that, I never brought it up again."

"What do you think might happen if you didn't have sex with him?" I asked her.

"I really like him, and I'm afraid he'll leave me for someone else—someone who will give him the sex."

Sonia's anxiety about her boyfriend breaking up with her was very real. Her body tensed up, her breathing grew labored, and her voice took on a higher pitch. Sonia had gotten accustomed to doing things that didn't feel in integrity with herself because she feared what might happen if she allowed herself to honor herself. Sadly, Sonia's story is not unique.

As Sonia walked through the practice of fierce authenticity, she learned more about herself. She developed the capacity to check in with herself. She realized there were times she enjoyed having sex with her partner and times when she wasn't interested. She learned to speak up for herself and say no. Sonia learned to tune into her soul's desire for her, rather than relying on outside sources to tell her what she should and shouldn't do. Much to Sonia's surprise, when she stopped abandoning herself and being driven by the fear that he might leave, and started living in integrity with herself, her relationship with her partner grew stronger.

"I used to be deathly afraid that he would break up with me if I didn't have sex with him, and it turns out, the more I practice being in integrity with myself, the more he honors and respects me!" Sonia exclaimed one day. "I actually feel closer to him now and the sex between us is amazing! Can you believe it, by learning to honor me and be true to myself, our relationship and our sex life has actually improved?"

"Yes, I can. That's what happens when we start to live in integrity with ourselves," I replied with a knowing smile on my face.

When you're in integrity with yourself, you stand by what feels right and true for you, no matter what. When you abandon yourself to make other people happy, you violate yourself. That puts you out of alignment with your integrity.

Choose to be in your integrity and notice how your relationships change.

VIOLATING BOUNDARIES

All too often, especially among women, there can be a tendency to unknowingly abandon yourself by over-giving and taking care of others before meeting your own needs. That leads you to feel angry and resentful, possibly without even realizing it. People who over-give often don't realize they need to set—and keep—boundaries. When you don't have boundaries, or the boundaries you do have are not strong, you feel constantly violated and as if you've abandoned yourself. It's hard to trust yourself if you're always abandoning yourself by violating your own boundaries and needs.

What does abandoning yourself look like? It might look like picking up the kids' toys even when you said you wouldn't, or taking on a co-worker's work even when they swore they would never ask you to again. It could look like not putting yourself to bed on time, even though you made a commitment to your health and well-being, or spending money on something when you just put yourself on a budget. Boundary violations make it really hard for parts of you to start, or keep, trusting you as a loving, caring, reliable ally and friend.

SHOWING UP AS YOURSELF

As you work to clear out the stories and limiting beliefs that have gotten in the way of who you authentically are, it's time to go back and get deeper into the stories of who you believe yourself to be.

Let's dive back into the stories you tell yourself. When we live our lives based on the stories we pick up from others, it feels as though the world is against us, often reinforcing the negative stories and beliefs we have about ourselves. To learn who you authentically are, clear out the old stories. They're the false beliefs that prevent you from being authentic in who you are. When you sort through and clear out the old stories and evaluate them for their continued usefulness in your life, you begin the process of unbecoming everything you are not. When you unbecome everything you are not, you create the space to become who you truly are.

The clearing-out process isn't about making the old stories disappear so you can create new ones. It's about cultivating relationships with the false, outdated, untrue stories you have been telling yourself, so you can access the truth of who you actually are. After years and years of believing in false stories about yourself, seeing the true stories can be difficult.

I like to use the analogy of a mirror to help demonstrate this idea. Every untrue story you believe about yourself, based on the stories you either learned or deduced about yourself, becomes a layer of dust over what was once a clean, bright, and shiny mirror. The layers build up over time and you can no longer see the clean, beautiful mirror. The reflection it gives back is distorted by the accumulation of grime. Doing the work of uncovering each of the layers, or de-conditioning yourself of those beliefs, helps clean up the mirror. As you remove the layers, you begin to see your true beauty and brilliance, which has always been there, waiting for you.

My client Jessica initially reached out because she was afraid she was going to repeat an old pattern in her romantic life. She had been married before and divorced. Every relationship she had ever been in had been an abusive one. When she called me, she was in a relationship that was actually quite the opposite of her other relationships, and she was terrified she was going to mess it up.

"I've never been with a man like this," Jessica said.

"He's actually kind, he doesn't yell at me, he's not jealous of how I look or who I talk to. He takes an interest in me and my life—and this feels super-uncomfortable to me. I don't know what to do with it!" She went on to say, "I end up kind of freaking out and pushing him away, and I don't want to push him away. He's actually a really good guy. What's wrong with me?"

A good portion of our work together was about helping Jessica learn what was "wrong" with her. It was about learning what stories she had told herself about her ability to love and be loved based on her life experiences, many of which were tragic. Jessica shared stories of family dysfunction, sexual abuse, rape, and a history of being attracted to alcoholics and addicts. She shared stories of domestic violence, assault, and then deciding she was done allowing herself to be treated that way. She still didn't understand what it was that kept her from allowing love from a kind and gentle man into her life, despite that being what she craved most in her life.

Little by little, as the layers cleared away, Jessica saw more and more of her beauty and brilliance as an inherently good and worthy human being. Jessica began to realize she was worthy of acceptance as exactly who she is.

I recall the day we sat together, in a quiet, contemplative space, in which I was facilitating a guided visualization and energy healing exercise with Jessica. She described seeing a door: "It's like, there's this great big steel door, with a huge lock on it, and it is sealed completely shut. I'm scared to see what's behind that door." She paused, and then she said with a smile, "I have a feeling there's something good back there ... Yes, there is something good back there."

I simply smiled and nodded when I heard Jessica's words, because she was absolutely right.

By the time we wrapped up our session that day, Jessica had been able to open that door, just a tiny bit. And that's all she needed to do to allow the flow of her true beauty, her true innocence, and her true essence to start to slowly become a greater part of her day-to-day life. As she did, her life began to change.

Jessica's story shows us the magic that happens as you take the time to slowly uncover the layers which have covered up the true you. It took at least a year of muddling through the old layers of untrue stories until Jessica got to the point where she was able to recognize that an inherent worthiness lives within her.

"I feel so much joy in my life," she exclaimed one day. "I feel like I am able to make better decisions, and I no longer want to push this amazing man out of my life. I really believe I deserve a good man, who treats me and my children well, and is kind. As an added bonus of all this work we've been doing, I also have a better relationship with my children now! I'm no longer worried about them, bending over backward to fix, save, or rescue them. Today, I trust that they too have their own paths and they are being cared for, and they too have this innocence inside of them, which they can connect with as they are ready to access it. It feels amazing to live my life with this new perspective! Free from worry, free from the old stories, and simply allowing myself to flow and just be. It's incredible and I never thought it would be possible for me!"

Through the practice of fierce authenticity, Jessica's miracles are possible for you, too.

THE TRUTH ABOUT FEAR

A miracle is a shift in perspective from fear to love, as Marianne Williamson says when she teaches from *A Course in Miracles*. Any time you find yourself in fear, consider where you have fallen out of the energy of love. In the same way you develop stories about yourself that aren't true, you also pick up fears that often aren't true, either.

The stories and the fears go hand in hand. When you have a story of how unlovable you are, you fear there is truth in that statement. When you fear there might be truth in that statement, it creates a fear of experiencing your unlovability coming true. That fear further leads you to put on armor, put up your walls, shut love out, which then reinforce your story of how unlovable you are. When your armor and walls are further reinforced, and you further distance yourself from love, it appears as though the stories of your unlovability are true.

Every person I have ever worked with lives a life based in fear. I, too, used to find myself often living in fear—fear of failure, so never start; fear of being unlovable, so never allow yourself to love and be loved; fear of being powerful, so keep your light dim and your actions small.

Not all fear is bad. There's a reason fear exists. From an evolutionary perspective, when we were living out in the wild and saw large predators heading our way, our fear absolutely served a purpose: It told us to find safety. Today, we live in a very different world, but we still operate from that part of the brain. Somewhere, deep down inside, you've created a fear response to being loved, being accepted, being successful, and being powerful. You put up walls and *run* when the possibility of being loved, being accepted, being successful, and being powerful arises. This is toxic fear—fear that has morphed from being a productive, healthy, evolutionary response to fear that has become constricting, restricting, and based in illusions due to the false stories you have created about yourself.

Part of the practice of fierce authenticity and cultivating a deeply intimate relationship with yourself is about learning whether there is truth or validity to your fears. Are they real fears based on your actual survival, or are they toxic fears, based on the false stories you have created about yourself?

When you are in fear, you might also feel lack. What I mean by lack is that "not-enough" feeling: not good enough, not pretty enough, not smart enough, not skinny enough, not witty enough, not funny enough, not enough money, not enough resources, not enough love, not enough of whatever it is for you.

When you feel lack in one area, it can bleed into other areas. When my former client Mary felt lack in her finances and the fear of not having enough money, it also translated into a feeling of lack in her relationships. All of a sudden, a highly functioning woman who surely had enough money and love available to her would become triggered and spin out into stories of not-enoughness.

"Shirani, I don't know how we're going to make the mortgage with the new increase in property taxes and everything due this month!" she frantically said to me. "It just sucks. I don't know what I'm going to do! And then my friends haven't been inviting me out, and I'm starting to wonder what's up with them. Are they pushing me out or something? And my husband, he's been distant and I'm worried he's going to ask for a divorce." Mary would rattle out her not-enoughs as she spun out in fear from financial triggers.

I paused her gently, saying, "You know, Mary, I've noticed we have a similar conversation a few times a year when you get triggered by financial fears. I'm wondering what's up with that?"

"Oh," Mary paused. "You're right." She thought some more and then said, "When I start to go into fear about my finances, I spin out about every other area in my life where I still feel I'm not good enough. There are times I feel like I'm not a good-enough friend because of all of my work and domestic tasks, then there are times I feel like I'm not a good-enough wife because I feel like I could do more or be more. Ohmigosh, you are so right! I do this every single time. When I feel lack in finances due to financial fear, all of a sudden, my entire perspective goes into lack!"

That's the way fear and lack work hand in hand to help keep you out of alignment with who you truly are. Anytime you find yourself in a "not-enough" thought pattern, take a pause and ask yourself, "Where am I feeling a lack?" After you evaluate where you are feeling a sense of lack, ask yourself, "Am I truly standing in all of my power and the Truth of who I authentically am?" These are two of the most-powerful questions you can ask yourself when you are working toward healing fear and lack. Not surprisingly, when you ask yourself these questions, you might realize that the stories of your wound are what's leading you to feel your sense of fear and lack. This is the toxic fear.

TUNING INTO YOURSELF

Now that you have started getting clarity about your stories, your fears, and the areas where you feel you lack, we can start to work on cultivating who you are, free from illusions. You will begin to take your relationship with yourself one step further as you cultivate a deeply intimate relationship with yourself.

You are a highly intuitive being. All humans are. You always know what feels like truth for you at your core. You always get a hunch when something isn't going well. You always know, yet it's likely you've been programmed out of connection with your own inner knowing, your own inner guidance system. You have been taught to rely instead on your head, your brain, your mind, and sources of information outside yourself. The problem with that approach is these will often play tricks on you when you don't allow them to also be connected with your body and your heart.

When your head is disconnected from your heart and

body, you can become too hard, cold, logistical, logical, and emotionless. When your heart is disconnected from your head, you can become too emotional, boundary-less, enmeshed with others, and concerned with pleasing others to your detriment. When both your head and your heart are connected with one another, you can navigate life with more peace, grace, and ease in your life. This happens because when your head and your heart are working in conjunction with one another, you are connected to a source of strength that can only be experienced when both are working in collaboration.

The practices of mindfulness and meditation are effective in getting control over your mind, harnessing its power, so you can create space for your heart and your body to operate in partnership with your brain. Mindfulness and meditation are exercises in mind-training. They allow you to slow down and become an observer of the thoughts and associated feelings that pass through your mind at rapid speed. They also allow you to become a centered and grounded spectator so you don't get caught up in a maelstrom of the thoughts that come at you from all angles at what can sometimes feel like lightning speed.

Once you work toward harnessing the thoughts that constantly race through your head, your heart will then have the room it needs to function as part of your whole being. The intersection of the head and the heart is that still, quiet place deep within you that always feels peace and always knows what's right and true for you. At that juncture lies the answers to any and all questions that arise in your life, and it is always accessible to you. You simply need to cultivate a relationship with it. Often, I hear people saying, "So-and-so is super-intuitive, I wish I could be that intuitive." My response is always, "You have access to the same intuition within you; you only need to cultivate the practice."

As you learn to rely on the wisdom that lies in the stillness of the quiet space within you, you will begin to feel a sense of ease as you make decisions throughout your day. All of a sudden, you will know exactly where to go, exactly what to do, exactly what to say and to whom. You won't experience the anxiety-provoking waffling you have become accustomed to. Instead, you will feel a deep peace and simply *know*. What used to once baffle you no longer will.

It's in this deep inner knowing that you will have greater self-awareness of your fiercely authentic self. Your exercise in further developing fierce authenticity and cultivating a deeper relationship with yourself is to begin a mindfulness and meditation practice. That's the way to continue cultivating a relationship with who you are at the juncture of your head and your heart. It's from there you'll be able to tune in and not only trust your own perceptions of who you are; you will also begin to trust your own perceptions of other people, places, and situations.

We are all born with this innate ability to tune into our innermost selves. As we grow, however, we lose connection with it. Either you learn to doubt yourself because the grown-ups around you are overtly telling you a duck is not a duck, even though you very clearly can see it is a duck, or you covertly pick up that it is not okay to connect with your own inner knowing. Part of the process of fierce authenticity is about allowing yourself to connect back to your own intuition, your own inner knowing, your own internal guidance system. As you learn how to do this, the rest of your life begins to flow with greater ease.

YOUR VALUES

Cultivating a relationship with yourself isn't complete without also evaluating what you value. The practice of connecting with yourself at the intersection between your head and your heart will allow you to tune into what your values are. Not the values that were placed upon you or were expected of you, rather, what your values are for you. You might find that some of what you value today is based in what you were taught or what you adapted. That's okay.

You might also find some of your values are different today than the ones you grew up with. That's okay, too. You are a grown individual. You have every right to decide what works for you, what you value, and what doesn't work for you. As you work on tuning into yourself, your values will become clearer to you.

Once you become familiar with what your values are, you will be able to use them to guide and inform your life. One of the challenges I see people face, especially women, is being unhappy about their lives because they aren't clear about their values. The flip side of that is women who say they value certain things, yet their choices and their decisions show something else. That's where the conflict within the self occurs and makes it difficult for you to access your authenticity.

Part of tapping into authenticity means living in alignment with what is right and true for you. When you stand in your commitment to fierce authenticity, you stand in Truth. It is in occupying the space of your Truth that your life changes in magical and miraculous ways.

Part of doing your best means looking at your life to identify your values and whether you are living your life based on them. If your life today doesn't include the values you think are important to you, reconsider them. Are they truly your values, or are they just things you think you should value, based on what others have told you?

LIVING IN FIERCE ALIGNMENT

The process of cultivating fierce authenticity means healing and clearing. It's an opportunity to learn who you are, where your stories and your fears have come from, what you value, what's been in alignment and what has not. Now it's time for you to look at the meaning of living in fierce alignment with yourself.

Before living my life in alignment, with my own inner knowing deep at the intersection of my head and my heart, I constantly looked for validation and approval outside myself. Whatever anyone else thought, I would jump on it. If I knew a relationship or a job was not in alignment with me but others said it was, I wouldn't care. I used to abandon myself and my own inner knowing, and ask everyone I knew what they thought instead. Then I would give their thoughts and opinions greater weight than my own inner knowing, further invalidating myself. I allowed others to completely dictate the direction in which I was to go.

As I began living my life in alignment with my own internal guidance system, my confidence in myself grew. More often than not, I made the choice to stay with myself rather than abandon myself. I experienced less anxiety, because I placed less weight on what others thought and relied instead on my own inner knowing. Of course, I still sought support from mentors and therapists, because it's important to have people in our lives whom we can turn to and reason things out with. However, I was no longer relying on them to be my source of something greater than me. Instead, I allowed myself to connect with the wisdom that comes from connection within myself.

My foundation as a human being became more solid and unbreakable. I realized that I was no longer a lost leaf blowing in the wind; I was the strong solid trunk of an oak tree. I experienced more ease, more happiness, more connection, more love, and more joy in my life and my relationships.

That's the transformation that happens when you shift from relying on external sources for validation to checking in with yourself. You will no longer blow in the wind, stirred up with anxiety, trying to get everyone to stamp your validation card. You will instead be solid and stable in your core. Life will still happen and unpleasant moments will still arise, and when they do, you will find that you are able to navigate them with greater confidence and ease.

Being solid and stable doesn't mean you become rigid and inflexible—not at all. Rather, you can stay strong at your core, yet remain flexible enough to move with whatever needs to move. If the branches didn't move, the tree would be so inflexible that it would break; it would either snap or get uprooted when a strong wind blows through. A tree needs both the solid trunk and supple branches that sway and move; both must work together.

As you work toward becoming deeply grounded within yourself and cultivate a nourishing and wholesome relationship with yourself, you will begin to feel this balance. Being solid and stable within yourself also means you honor yourself when something doesn't feel good or right to you. You make choices guided by your true self, rather than out of anxiety or fear. When you are in alignment with yourself, grounded in who you are, you no longer attempt to change yourself to get external validation. You no longer contort yourself into all sorts of different shapes to appease others. You remain aligned with what is right and true for you.

When you live the principles of fierce authenticity in your life, you experience self-confidence, and know you are enough just as you are. You no longer need to impress anyone because you know who you are at the center of your being, and you love and accept yourself exactly as you are. As you begin to believe you are enough as you are, and love and accept yourself for it, you will begin to experience the miracles of experiencing the healthy, loving relationships you desire. When you live in true alignment with who you authentically are and you allow yourself to stand fully in your Truth, doors will open for you. Your world will open up in a great big new way. You will know the miracles of allowing yourself to show up, be seen, and get love.

MEDITATION TO MEET YOUR
FIERCELY AUTHENTIC SELF

To help you get further into relationship with your fiercely authentic self, I have included a powerful healing meditation for you. This meditation will help you peel back the layers of what everyone has said you should be, what you should do, and how you should act, and get to the true essence of who you are underneath all of the roles and expectations others have placed on you. As you go through this meditation, be aware that new expectations, roles, and voices might arise in your awareness. If they do, just go with them. If you wish, you can record this meditation as you speak it out aloud, then go back and listen to it again.

For this meditation, sit comfortably in a chair with your feet flat on the floor and your back upright. Whenever you are ready, you may close your eyes to allow for the full healing experience.

Start by releasing all of the air from your lungs and then taking in a nice, deep, fresh inhale through your nose. Then, slowly and gently exhale that breath through your mouth.

Next, take three deep cleansing breaths—inhaling through your nose all the way down to your belly, as you count to four in your mind; hold that breath in your belly for a count of seven, and then very slowly and gently exhale through your mouth to the count of eight. This is a 4-7-8 breathing pattern. Repeat this pattern two more times on your own.

When you have completed your three cleansing breaths, gently close your lips and breathe slowly and naturally through your nose.

Now, give your mind permission to relax. Let your mind know that for the next 10 minutes or so, there is nowhere to go and nothing to do. Simply allow the meditation to guide you to your fiercely authentic self.

To help you become more present in your body, feel your feet as they touch the floor. Feel your body as it sits supported in the chair. Feel your hands and whatever they might be resting on. Notice the temperature of the room and any other sensations you might feel on your skin. Don't try to change anything; simply become more present with your body.

Now take a moment to think about all of the different roles you have been assigned in your life: daughter, sister, student, employee, boss, CEO, spouse, lover, mother, friend …

Next, think about all the different messages you have received about yourself. What were the messages and where did they come from? Whose voices were in your head telling you these things about you? Take some time now to think about these.

Now, I invite you to start taking off all of these different roles and removing all of these messages from the inner vision of your mind. See yourself as, one by one, you take off each and every role you have ever been assigned, every expectation that others have ever placed on you, and every negative message you have ever received about yourself. As you picture yourself taking off all of these different roles, feel their weight lifted off you. Feel the lightness that is you when you free yourself from everything that is not authentically you.

When you remove all the roles, expectations, and messages, you are left standing as your true, authentic self, free from outside influences. You are now free to live based purely on who you are at your innermost core.

Picture your authentic self standing before you and look closer. Who is this woman? What does she like? How does she dress? How does she behave? What does she value? What is important to her? What activities does she enjoy? What brings her joy and contentment?

Take a few moments to stand with this woman, allowing her full expression to emerge. This woman who stands before you now is you as your fiercely authentic self.

As you stand before this woman, imagine what your life would be like if you allowed yourself to live as her. How would your life be different? How would it be better? Picture all of the ways your life would be changed if you allowed yourself to live as this full expression of yourself.

When you are ready, I invite you to step into this woman—you—and to feel yourself coming into your body and your being. This woman is your true expression of yourself. Feel yourself fully stepping into and embracing this woman. Allow this woman to permeate into every single cell of your body. Allow yourself to merge with her and to become her. She is not a role, she is not a mirage, she is not an illusion or an image; she is your highest, innermost, most-authentic self.

As you step into this fiercely authentic expression of yourself, I invite you to carry her with you and allow her to guide you to live your day-to-day life as she would—in every aspect of your life. As you feel this new sensation, take time to pause, take a few deep breaths, and let it fully sink in.

Now that you have connected with your fiercely authentic self, it's time for you to come back to the present moment.

Begin by feeling your feet as they rest on the floor. Feel your body as it sits supported in the chair. Know that just as this chair supports you, your deeper self always supports you throughout your life. You have cultivated a deeply intimate and unshakeable relationship with yourself. And you are here.

Start to feel your hands and whatever they are resting on. Notice the temperature of the room and any other sensations on your skin. You can start to wriggle your fingers, wriggle your toes, take a stretch, and whenever you are ready, bring your full attention back to this present moment.

You can download a bonus version of this meditation at www.fierceauthenticity.com.

BEING A BEACON OF LIGHT

In my experience, when women work through the processes I've shared with you, each one realizes she is indeed a powerful woman, full of so much joy that her cup overflowed to those around her. She learns it's okay to do the things she enjoys doing and to stop hiding behind a façade. When each of these women taps into who she is as her fiercely authentic self, the way she carries herself changes and her inner light shines more brightly. She becomes a beacon of light, drawing other joyful and authentic people to her.

These women's lives become richer and fuller. By tapping into their fiercely authentic selves and living in alignment with them, these women share their true selves with the world and are finally able to form healthy, loving bonds with others.

Through the solid foundation of fierce love for yourself and fierce care of yourself, your authenticity has room to grow and flourish. When living authentically, you live according to what you believe—no longer according to the false illusions and limiting beliefs that others have placed on you. Once you emerge solid in who you are and what you stand for, you remain stable and grounded in yourself, while still remaining flexible to life's ups and downs.

By developing a fiercely loving and caring relationship with yourself, you have cultivated a deeply intimate relationship with yourself, which allows you to experience loving, caring, authentic relationships with others. You can allow yourself to show up, be seen, and get love. Ultimately, that's what the entire process of fierce authenticity is about.

Once you get this far, you're able to move to the next part of the practice: fierce communication of your Truth. In the next chapter, you will learn how fierce love for yourself, fierce care of yourself, and fierce authenticity come together to help you fiercely communicate in a way that is gentle, nurturing, and loving, while still remaining true to who you are. You will learn to share your Truth without intentionally or unintentionally seeking to harm others. The great Buddhist monk Thich Nhat Hanh says most often we hurt others not because we are trying to be malicious, but rather because of our unskillfulness.

5

FIERCE COMMUNICATION
(of Your Truth)

To truly communicate, we must take re-
sponsibility for the heart space that exists
between us and another.
—Marianne Williamson

One of the most beautiful gifts you can give yourself and others around you is the gift of communicating your authentic truth with love, care, kindness, and compassion.

One of the miracles that occurs when you are able to fiercely communicate your truth is you find it no longer matters how others respond. You'll feel good about simply honoring yourself and giving voice to your needs, wants, and concerns.

Others value and honor you at the level you value your-self. When you learn to honor and value yourself at a high-er level, others will follow you upward. Your relationships will shift in a big and miraculous way.

Take Jeanette as an example. The mother of two small children, Jeanette wasn't happy with the way she had been treating them. She told me, "I'm so tired and burnt out that I end up snapping at my sweet, innocent little children. I don't like it. I see the look of terror in their eyes when I do so and I literally watch them shrink away from me. I need help. I don't want to treat them like this anymore."

As we began working together, little by little, Jeannette began incorporating the principles of fierce love for herself and fierce care of herself into her life. She noticed she was now able to be more present with herself, which led her to stop snapping at her children and start communicating with love and care instead.

"It's amazing," she exclaimed one day, "I actually enjoy my kids today! I'm not in a constant state of panic over 'what do they want from me now?' When I'm with them, I actually feel myself operating from a space of love and care for them. Do they still do some stupid stuff? Absolutely. And am I able to be more patient and tolerant with them? Yes. Oh, what a world of difference it makes!"

Jeanette isn't the only woman who has shared the miraculous shifts she's experienced as she has learned to cultivate the practice of fierce authenticity to guide her life. Perla was better able to communicate with her teammates. Sandra was able to show up as her fiercely authentic self in romantic relationships. Kayla stopped isolating her friends with cutting remarks. Every single one of these women experienced a transformation in the way they were able to show up and communicate in the world.

Without getting to know who you authentically are and how to express that in the world, you don't know what it is you even want to communicate to others. Messages get mixed, wires get crossed, signals get scrambled—clarity gets lost. You attract people and situations into your life that reflect back your lack of clarity.

A big part of the communication problem we may face is having lived in the story of our wounding for far too long. The only skill we learned was how to communicate from our wound. When I used to believe in the stories of how unworthy I was, I communicated based on how unworthy I thought I was. My external reality and how I navigated life were driven by the false compass of my supposed unworthiness.

As you become more familiar with your wounds and learn how to tend to yourself when old stories arise, you will become more skillful in your ability to communicate with more love, care, and authenticity in your life. While you're in the midst of clearing those wounds, you might still stumble and fall, like a baby learning to walk. You're in new territory. You're using wobbly baby legs to navigate a terrain that you've only viewed before from your butt-scoot angle of the world.

Once you've been able to wobble through and master fierce love for yourself, fierce care of yourself, and fierce authenticity, you'll soon experience a mastery that allows you to run with those newfound legs. You'll find yourself more able and excited to show up and be seen, and as a result, you will find yourself getting more love.

VERBAL VERSUS NONVERBAL COMMUNICATION

How you say things is equally as important as how you express yourself through nonverbal communication. We all know that nonverbal communication includes body language, such as puffing yourself up or shrinking yourself down, giving a smile, or rolling your eyes. But nonverbal communication goes beyond what your physical body does. It includes other expressions of yourself, such as the way you do your hair, the way you dress, what brands you wear, what books you read, and what hobbies you enjoy.

Remember Meena? She was the woman who didn't

know what she liked to eat, what her own favorite style of clothing was, or what her favorite colors were when we began our work together. She had no idea! By the time she got into a deeply intimate relationship with herself, she discovered she loves Thai food and hates Mexican food. She discovered she feels fiercely feminine and sexy when she wears flowing dresses and shirts that shift with her body. She discovered she enjoys bright, bold colors. Meena also discovered hobbies beyond her children! One day, Meena came to our session with a brand-new cell phone cover.

"Shirani, I made this!" she exclaimed with excitement.

One of Meena's assignments as she was getting to know herself was to allow herself to explore her creativity. When she did, she discovered she had a knack for creating cell phone charms and decals.

"I had no idea that I'm so creative!" she continued with a beaming smile on her face. "I always thought I was boring, that I wasn't creative, that I was all about logic and algorithms. Turns out, my right brain needs space to express itself, too. Now I see those stories I used to tell myself as complete lies. Lies—each and every single one of those stories was limiting beliefs about who I am and who I am capable of being. I feel so free knowing that I have a whole set of gifts and talents I never knew I had! And that's not all," she added, "I've also discovered I'm good at making natural skincare products, so I've launched an online store for people to buy my creations. This is so exciting! I've never felt so sure of myself before!"

Meena was beside herself with excitement. Her glow lit up the room. It was a gift to witness Meena's transformation as she uncovered what was true for her and allowed herself to express herself in a myriad of ways. Everything from her clothing to the colors she wore, to the way she carried herself had changed. When Meena and I first began our work together, she always sat back in her seat, making herself small, as though she was trying to be unseen. The day Meena shared this news with me, she carried herself upright with confidence and had an air of lightness about her. Meena's nonverbal communication demonstrated that she was a woman who allowed herself to connect fiercely to her authenticity, which included connecting with her creativity. She was now aglow with a self-assuredness that was clearly visible.

To develop a greater awareness of your own nonverbal communication, I encourage you to take three to five communication checkpoints during the day. In your checkpoints, ask yourself, "is the way I am nonverbally communicating an authentic expression of who I am?" If your answer is yes, continue on with your day. If your answer is no, ask yourself, "where have I fallen out of alignment with myself and what do I need to tend to within me to return to a fierce expression of myself?"

FIERCE RESPECT FOR YOURSELF

How many times have you found yourself thinking, "What will he say if I do this?" "What will she think if I say that?" "What will they think of me if I don't go to their dinner party?" When all your words and actions are based on what other people say or think about you, you are abandoning yourself and giving others too much power. You take yourself out of the equation. Your entire experience becomes about what others will say and think about you, based on what you say or do.

What others think of you is none of your business.

Others will always have an opinion of you: how you dress, your hairstyle, how you walk, what you say, what you eat, and everything else. When you cultivate a deeply intimate and loving relationship with yourself, others' opinions no longer hold the weight they once did in your life. The freedom you experience will be liberating!

No longer will you bend backward, forward, sideways, and twist yourself into a pretzel to appease others. Instead, you'll operate through fierce love and care for yourself and others, based on the expression of your fiercely authentic self. When you do that, your life miraculously changes. People will have greater respect for you, and more importantly, you will have greater respect for yourself.

When you possess this level of self-respect, the world around you changes. In the beginning, the changes might not look pleasant, because when you stop pleasing people, people won't be pleased. As you stay with the process, though, you'll find your footing and will be able to run and play in the world in a whole new way, a way that allows you to be responsible for yourself.

Being Responsible to and for Yourself

One day I received a call from Titi. She was at her wits' end trying to do and be everything for everybody. Her life had become unmanageable and she knew it.

"Shirani, I need help. My kids constantly need something from me, my husband puts all these demands on me, my parents live locally and they always ask me to do things as well. I just can't take it anymore. If something doesn't change, I'm going to snap!"

Titi was the oldest of three children. She was "the responsible one." Her parents were immigrants to this country and as the eldest, as soon as she was old enough, she was put in charge and made responsible for her siblings.

"To help make ends meet, my parents both worked two jobs when they moved here and they required me to cook, to clean, to go to school, to do my homework, to help my siblings with their chores, and to make sure their homework was done as well. It was a lot to handle. I was only a kid! I never got to do the fun things my friends did. I wasn't allowed to go out, and I had to stay home to take care of everybody and everything. Even now, they still expect me to be the one to take care of everything. I have two other siblings, yet anytime my parents want anything, they always come to me. Then add my own kids, my husband, my own responsibilities in my household today, and it's just too much. I can't keep doing this anymore. My blood pressure is high, I'm always feeling stressed, my anxiety is through the roof. This isn't sustainable anymore."

As we continued exploring what life was like for Titi, the theme over and over again was about over-responsibility for others and not enough responsibility for herself. When I asked Titi how she takes care of herself, she looked at me as though I was an alien with two heads. When I asked her how she shows love to herself, again, the same puzzled look. When asked who she was and what she liked, she said, "I never got a chance to even think about that for myself!"

Titi is a classic example of a woman who does for others at her own expense. As a result, the others in her life didn't respect her wants, needs, and desires—and she had lost all respect for herself as well. The people who love you may still take your love and use it for their own purposes. Learning to respect yourself and how to lovingly communicate your respect for yourself to others is of the utmost importance.

Every single woman I have ever worked with tells me that when she starts to demonstrate respect for herself, the people in her life finally begin respecting her, too. When you are responsible to yourself by setting and honoring boundaries, when you know who you authentically are and how you wish to show up in the world, you demonstrate respect for yourself.

By demonstrating fierce respect for yourself, you communicate to others how to have respect for you, too.

HARNESSING THE POWER OF WORDS

Words are powerful. What you do with them matters. How you use them matters, too. Words can make or break you and the life you're creating. No conversation about how we communicate would be complete without addressing how to harness the power of our words. When you practice fierce authenticity, you're learning a way to cultivate the use of your words for the purposes of love and healing. Fierce communication includes healing the ways you use your words, so that you can speak more love into our world.

Living in the Present to Create a Different Future

When we continue to live past experiences in the present moment, we block our ability to create a different future.

When you're trying to break old patterns, telling the same old story with the same old energy isn't going to help you get the love you want. Instead, be mindful of how you choose to tell your story. One of the most powerful ways is to focus on what it used to be like versus how it is now. When you're able to focus on how it's different now, then you'll be able to create a reality that is different from your past.

Putting this into practice is simple. Think of the way things were in the past, and then change the language to how you want them to be now. The format is: "In the past, _____, and today _____." Fill in the blanks with thoughts, feelings, and behaviors of the past and the new thoughts, feelings, and behaviors you desire for the present and future. For example: "In the past, I used to take on my co-worker's tasks and feel resentful about it. And today, I feel good taking care of my own work, while allowing my co-worker to be responsible for herself."

Another example is: "In the past, I used to dishonor myself in my relationships with others. And today, I honor and respect myself first."

Notice the difference between the "in the past" sentences and the "and today" sentences. There is a powerful shift—one that allows you to take full ownership of your actions.

Being Authentic with Your Words

When you are authentic with your words, you mean what you say, say what you mean, and don't say it meanly. When you're struggling to be authentic, you might say things you don't mean, such as making empty promises just to appease somebody, or conversely, making empty threats in the hope of getting someone to do something. Either way, you are out of integrity with yourself and your words aren't authentic, because you are neither meaning what you say nor saying what you mean. The struggle to be authentic with our words can also include saying things in a mean and unloving way.

Rosa had a hard time with all three of these. She was taught to be docile. She was taught she couldn't share what she really thought and that she had to be agreeable, that she had to keep the peace and avoid making waves at any cost. These messages had a major impact on all of Rosa's relationships, especially with her teenage kids.

"My kids walk all over me. Whenever I ask them to do something, they end up ignoring me," Rosa said when we met.

"Can you share some examples with me?" I asked.

"I ask them to take out the trash, and they walk right past me. I tell them to clean up their rooms, and they keep playing with their phones. I tell them they need to make their own lunch for school, and they actually laugh at me and say 'Mom, that's your job.' I'm embarrassed to admit that my kids act this way with me."

"Ouch, that must hurt," I said. "And how do you respond when they act that way?"

"I end up yelling at them, telling them I'm going to send them to live with their dad, and then I feel bad. So I take out the trash, clean up their rooms, and pack up their lunch," Rosa said with her head down in defeat.

"Have you ever followed through on sending them to live with their dad?"

"No."

"And how does that affect your relationships with your children?"

"They take further advantage of me."

It was clear Rosa had a hard time saying what she meant, not making empty threats, and at times saying things in ways that weren't mean.

As Rosa dove into the practice of fierce communication, I encouraged her, saying, "Rosa, if you aren't going to send your kids off to live with their dad, you need to stop making empty threats about that. Doing so makes you less believable and less credible. You also need to stop doing the things you asked them to do. Leave the trash for them to take out. Leave their rooms a mess. Let them make their own lunch. Your actions speak louder than your words. If you keep doing the things you asked them to do, they get the message that it's okay for them to ignore you, brush you off, or outright laugh at you. They know you'll end up doing everything. No matter what, stand your ground. Don't give in to their whining or complaining!"

Rosa did as we discussed. After an initial period of trial and error, resistance, and return to old behavior, Rosa succeeded in communicating with her children through her words and her actions that she was serious.

"After weeks of back and forth, my children have finally begun to respect me! It's incredible! And you know what they told me? They told me they always knew it was their responsibility to do these things, but they insisted on not doing them because they knew I would eventually do them myself. It's amazing that when my words and my actions finally became consistent with one another, my children stepped up and started respecting me."

Rosa learned the lesson of honoring herself and communicating to others, both verbally and nonverbally, by being authentic with her words and consistent in her actions.

When you know who you are and what works for you, and you have love for yourself, it allows you to have love for others. That's when you can start to say what you mean, mean what you say, and not say it meanly.

One of the biggest challenges is when you don't yet have the love and care for yourself, and still don't know who you are. Then it's difficult to communicate effectively. Because she wasn't honoring herself, Rosa, like many others I have worked with, would say things she didn't mean, make empty threats, and at times even said and did things that were very mean. That was Rosa in the past. Today, Rosa has a different reality.

FIERCE TRUST IN YOURSELF

When you begin expressing yourself and communicating with fierce love, care, and authenticity, you'll also be cultivating the skill of knowing when and how to communicate.

Trust yourself as you learn. When the time to communicate is right, you'll know.

Many of us get caught up in the go-go-go mentality, thinking everything needs to be done yesterday. We discover something that makes us uncomfortable and we need a solution to take us out of our pain *yesterday*. We can't tolerate our discomfort and we can't tolerate the ambiguity of not solving the problem *now*. The pitfall with that is, when we react immediately, we make rash decisions based on fear of discomfort, rather than generating thoughtful responses. Reacting is one of the most dangerous actions we can take. Reactions cause the most damage in our relationships.

Take a moment to consider: Whenever you had a reaction based on your fear, how did it work out for you? Did it lead you to your desired outcome or did it instead leave you feeling worse inside?

For most people, the answer to this is, "It led me to feel good for the moment, then worse afterward."

When you instead take time to pause, to reflect, and to sit in the discomfort, only then will the best answers appear.

The problem is, when we learn something that feels uncomfortable, we have usually come upon some awareness of ourselves, our situation, our behavior—and we don't like it. We immediately jump to taking action so we can avoid the discomfort. When we do, we're bypassing a very important step: Acceptance.

One way to achieve positive outcomes is derived from 12-step principles: move through the three-step process of awareness, acceptance, and then action. In the awareness stage, you recognize that something has you feeling out of sorts. It could be the triggering of an old story or a belief in your not-enoughness. By bypassing the acceptance stage, you make uninformed decisions, which are reactions in disguise.

The acceptance part of this three-part process includes a feeling stage as well as an information-gathering stage. When you allow yourself to sit in acceptance, you accept your feelings and gather information around what purpose this thought, behavior, or situation has been serving for you. Once you have been able to feel your feelings and gather sufficient information, you can take the action step and make an informed decision about what your next move will be.

We may want to bypass acceptance, because accepting that we have been engaging in certain unproductive or negative thoughts, behaviors, or situations is often too much for us. We don't want to acknowledge that we have been creating most of the situations in our life ourselves. I have a dear friend who says "Awareness is a bitch," and on the flip side, "and you gotta love her." Awareness is a double-edged sword that invites you into a process of consciously engaging in a choice point: Keep doing things the way you have been doing them or choose to do things differently.

My client Monica is quite a hothead. When we began working together, her main concern was that her anger was getting the best of her and ruining her relationships.

"This anger is causing so much wreckage in my relationships. Anything can set me off. I get reactive and can't stop myself. Words come flying out, mean things get said, and while in the moment it feels satisfying, afterward I feel like shit," Monica told me when we first met.

"What happens when you get into that reactive place?"

"I don't know. It's like something sets me off, some button gets pushed, and I'm not even there anymore. All of a sudden, someone else is inside me saying these mean things to people."

As Monica started cultivating the practice of fierce authenticity, she realized that the wall of anger that came in and blocked her off was a protective response. She had built it inside to help her not have to risk being hurt in her relationships. It didn't matter who she was responding to—romantic relationships, friends, co-workers, family, her go-to protective mechanism was anger. She had experienced tremendous hurt in the past, and anger was the best way she knew to keep herself from getting hurt again.

Monica learned it was best to be the first to lash out, the first to harm. Unfortunately, this story led her to lash out in fear and to self-protect, then feel bad afterward. It was a vicious cycle. She wanted out.

One of the most helpful tools for Monica was learning to take a pause. She cultivated a mindfulness/quiet time practice, which allowed her to cultivate a relationship with her own inner knowing and to develop fierce trust in what's right for her.

"Shirani, I feel so much peace in my life," she said one day. "Hectic things still happen in my life, and I feel peace. I don't lash out at people anymore, and they are blown away by my ability to stay calm and rational with them. When someone says or does something that triggers me, I have the ability to take a pause, check in with myself, get familiar with what scared parts of myself are feeling, and then make a mindful decision about how I'm going to respond. Doing this has led to miracles in my life!

"I seriously used to be the fuel tanker that fueled fires, and today, that no longer happens. I feel so much better as a result of it! I'm not leaving behind a trail of wreckage, and the people in my life respond differently to me. I know what to say, and how to say it, when my inner guidance tells me it's time to say it. It's been miraculous!"

As Monica shared her story, I saw her inner light glowing. The hard, tough exterior she had built around her had slowly been crumbling down as she healed layer after layer of her internal stories. The more she took ownership for herself, her stories, and her own life, the more she was able to navigate the world with dignity and with grace.

"And the best part is," Monica added, "the people in my life actually respect me today, not out of fear like they used to, but out of genuine love. They aren't afraid of my reactions anymore; they actually have deep respect for me. That has opened up a whole new world for me."

DIFFICULT CONVERSATIONS

I want to leave you with a word about difficult conversations. One of the biggest challenges I see in my practice and in the lives of those around me, myself included, is the tendency to avoid engaging in difficult conversations. Most of us think it will be too painful to have a difficult conversation with someone, so we continue to endure the situation that leads us to pain. We deny, neglect, and ignore our own inner knowing to avoid the pain. You might have a feeling your partner is cheating on you, or that your child is using their allowance to purchase marijuana. You sense that something is seriously wrong in your relationships, but rather than facing the situation through the practice of fierce authenticity, you choose to ignore the inner nudge, the pain, in an attempt to avoid it. Before you know it, ten years have passed and it comes out that your husband wants a divorce because he has been cheating on you, or your child ends up in a costly rehab facility because you didn't address the situation sooner.

Difficult conversations are difficult for a reason: they're painful in the moment. However, the pain of avoiding and prolonging a difficult conversation only makes it worse for you in the long run. When difficult situations need to be addressed and conversations need to be had, make the loving, caring, and authentic choice to implement fierce communication of what needs to be said. As you practice the tools given to you in this book, you will be well-equipped to handle any situation or conversation that comes your way. You will be able to navigate them with dignity and grace. Remember that miracles arise when you shift your perspective from fear to love.

6

TRANSITIONS
(the Fiercely Authentic Way)

You must love in such a way
that the person you love feels free.
—*Thich Nhat Hanh*

I f you've been implementing the ideas I suggest in this book, you're probably experiencing some shifts, or transitions, in your relationships. When you start implementing boundaries and when you start prioritizing yourself over others, those others might not be pleased. It might cause some temporary upset and discomfort as your relationship patterns change.

Don't give up or stop doing the work. Upset and discomfort in your relationships means the changes you're making are working!

Nobody likes change. We resist it with a passion. Parts of us make it their sole job to ensure we stay the same, our circumstances stay the same, and our feelings stay the same (even when those feelings are uncomfortable ones). Change can be terrifying. It means letting go of things you know and are comfortable to you, and swimming out into new and unknown waters. When we're the ones changing, we're scared—and those around us get scared, too.

Remember that miracles are a shift in perception from fear to love. When you can recognize that both you and those around you are scared of the changes that are happening, you can respond with love: love for yourself and love for them. What is most-loving and kind for you is *always* what is most-loving and kind for everyone involved.

Transitions are perpetually occurring because change is perpetually occurring. Buddhism and other Eastern philosophies teach the only constant in life is change. Change is the only thing you can count on. You are an ever-evolving, ever-growing being. Remaining the same without change leads to stagnation. Eventually, life stops feeling good. The energy of stagnation is dull, sludgy, and unfulfilling. Think of a pool of stagnant water. It's covered with pond scum, full of mosquitoes, and it stinks.

Humans aren't meant for stagnation. Stagnation leads to decay. Learn to get comfortable with transitions. Get comfortable with change. And be gentle with yourself in the process.

TYPES OF TRANSITIONS

Some transitions occur within yourself; others occur within your relationship while you are still in it; and others occur that lead to a completion of the relationship. All of these transitions change the relationship as a whole. Facing transitions in your relationships doesn't mean what you have been doing isn't working. It means quite the opposite: It means everything you have been doing has been working quite well!

The transitions that happen within yourself are those leading to a change in your own inner world: your thoughts, feelings, and perceptions about who you are and how you wish to be treated, the ways in which you show up for yourself, and the way you allow others to show up for you. These inner changes lead to a shift in the relationship within yourself and have nothing to do with anyone else, other than the way you communicate with others, through both your words and your actions.

The transitions that occur within your relationships

while you are still in them might cause a temporary shake-up, until the other person is able to up-level with you. Up-leveling happens every time you make a shift and a change to better yourself and elevate yourself to a new way of being. The person you are in a relationship with (regardless of who the person is—partner, parent, child, sibling, boss, friend) usually manages to find a way to meet you at your new level. In the interim, there might be a temporary upset, because you have thrown off the balance of the relationship as you both knew it.

Rosa, whom you met earlier, experienced this type of transition. Rosa's children weren't happy with her when she began refusing to do for them what they could do for themselves. They didn't like that she wouldn't make them lunch anymore, even though they were fully capable human beings. They resisted, they fought her on it, they fought the change itself. As Rosa stuck with herself throughout her process, though, her relationship with her children eventually shifted and a new balance was created: Her children not only took care of themselves, they also began respecting her.

The final type of transition is when, despite your best efforts and the best efforts of the person you are in a relationship with, the up-level can't happen. One or the other decides it's time to leave. This is most common in romantic partnerships, but it also happens in work relationships, with friends, and even with family members. This type of transition is often the most difficult to handle.

NAVIGATING TRANSITIONS

Navigating the transition when a relationship of any sort—be it romantic, work, family, or friends—comes to an end is hard. Rarely are both people in a relationship in agreement about when it has to end. Learning how to navigate these types of transitions with dignity and grace is essential to the process of fierce authenticity. You've been navigating the first two types of transitions as you've been working through this book. Now it's time to learn how to navigate this final type of transition, in a fiercely loving, caring, and authentic way.

Think back to the person you were when you picked up this book. With all the knowledge and insight you've gained, are you still the same person you were? Or are you now a person who is already navigating life with more fierceness, dignity, and grace? Now it's time to apply the same dignity and grace to relationships that need to transition out.

Remember Sandra? The marketing executive who used to spin out about everything in her personal life even though she had it all together in her work world? When she began working with me, she didn't understand how to navigate transitions. They were a continual struggle for her. They constantly left her feeling emptier and more alone than she had felt before she got into the relationship.

Sandra learned to navigate her life and the various transitions in it with tremendous love and dignity.

"We broke up and I actually felt so much peace around it," she said after a break-up. "I used to feel like there was something wrong with me when a relationship ended. It used to feed the stories of my not-enoughness. Today, I know that I really gave this relationship my best, as did he. He gave it the best he could do, and that best just didn't work for me and our relationship. Today, I have so much love for him as a person, I truly wish him well, and I know he wasn't right for me. And that's okay."

I could feel the peace emanating from Sandra as she shared those words. We had talked about a number of her other break-ups during our work together. What I heard from Sandra that day confirmed she had truly learned the lessons outlined in this book. She was a transformed woman.

The same was true of Annette when she finally made the decision to leave her job. She used to feel chaos and pressure about changing careers, because she constantly wondered what others, in particular her parents, would think of her. She had fears of being called a failure. Leaving the profession she had studied for to go into a completely different field was something Annette could only ever dream of doing.

"I was able to tell my family the work I was doing, I wasn't doing for me. I was doing it for them," she said one day. "I was able to tell them that I never enjoyed that field of study and only did it because I thought that's what they wanted of me." Annette went on with tears in her eyes, "After their initial shock about my quitting my job, my parents told me they're proud of me for finally stepping up and doing something for me. It was one of the most joyful, honest, authentic, and loving moments I have ever experienced with my family. It felt so good."

Kayla had a similar experience when one of her friends decided to end their friendship, despite Kayla's best efforts to shift the relationship.

"It really hurts that Wendy chose to end our friendship," Kayla said to me after the friend had been nonresponsive to her attempts to connect. "She was a great friend. I get it, though—she's going through a lot of her own stuff. I'm sure my negativity when I snapped at her repeatedly didn't help. Today, I can feel the pain and sadness of the relationship ending without feeling like there's something wrong with me. Today, I can feel the pain and sadness without making frantic attempts to reconnect to make sure she's okay. Today, I recognize that I can feel hurt, and still be okay, regardless of where she is in her process. Today, I have tools for me. And today, I can identify the gifts and the blessings from my friendship with Wendy."

Each of these women was able to choose a different response from the ones they previously would have when they were operating from their childhood stories of not-enoughness. They had come into a greater relationship with and healed parts of themselves that operated in stories of woundedness, lovelessness, and not-enoughness. Each of these women was able to navigate these transitions with dignity and grace. They were able to feel peace. They were able to feel sadness. They were able to feel pain. And they were able to know that despite it all, they were still okay. Most importantly, they knew they would remain okay because they believed they were worthy and valuable human beings.

LOVE IS ALL THERE IS

"Oh, my gosh, I finally get it!" exclaimed Vivian one day. "This whole time, while I was in the story of how not good enough I thought I was, all I could see was how terrible the woman my husband cheated on me with was. She was the villain and I was the victim. That's the way I told myself the story, over and over again. All the tears, all the sleepless nights, obsessing over how this woman was the devil, and it turns out, she was really here to teach me something about myself."

I watched Vivian as the light bulbs began to go on in her head. She realized that all the pain she subjected herself to over her husband's infidelity was based in the false story she had about her unlovability.

"She helped me to uncover all of these stories I had about how unworthy and unlovable I thought I was. If my husband hadn't had this affair, I could have continued on living the status quo life with him, never truly knowing who I am. Instead, because he cheated on me and I was so livid, I found my way here, where you helped me learn all of my stories and how I used to play them out over and over in my life. She wasn't the devil. She was more like a master teacher, here to teach me about myself!"

I watched as Vivian's excited "Eureka!" face slowly softened and her breath came back to a gentle rise and fall. "Wow, in realizing that, I actually have a lot of gratitude for this woman. If it weren't for her, I wouldn't be here as truly, authentically me today," Vivian said softly, with a tear rolling down her cheek. "I would still be playing out the stories of my not-enoughness and wondering why my life sucked. This whole time, I thought it was always about her, and in this moment I realize that it was never about her. It was about me all along."

With that powerful awareness, Vivian completed her work with me.

In the world we live in today, in which fear runs rampant, I believe all of us are here to learn the lessons of love and forgiveness. We are all here to learn the ways in which we keep love out, build walls around ourselves, and operate with hate and indifference for each other and ourselves. Through cultivating the practice of fierce authenticity you shift your experience, shift your perspective, and move into a world filled with more love. Because ultimately, love is all there is.

My purpose in writing this book initially was to help individuals learn how to experience more love in their lives. As I walked my clients through this work and began writing this book, it became more and more evident that I was writing it for a more-global purpose: to help all of us clear the blocks that keep us in fear and keep the world the seemingly loveless place it is. When one of us does this work, we make a ripple effect which, in turn, invites more love into the world. The movement of bringing more love into the world is a grassroots movement, a movement that starts at home, no matter how painful it might feel at times.

FORGIVENESS

A brief word on forgiveness. Just as you can't do a bypass around the acceptance, awareness, and action process, you can't bypass the middle parts of the path toward forgiveness. There's tons of fluff floating around out there instructing you to "just forgive." The reality for most is that when you don't honor the difficult experiences and the difficult feelings, and allow your frozen feelings to thaw out, you are simply setting yourself up for temporary relief.

Forgiveness is a process that starts with becoming aware of what transpired, sometimes for the first time ever and sometimes from a deeper perspective. Then forgiveness moves through the acceptance phase, including all of your feelings about it, and it comes into the action phase, of deciding what you are going to do about it now. When any part of the process is bypassed, you are at risk of the feelings still lingering unresolved within you, waiting for just the right moment to rear their heads and sabotage you. You've come too far on your journey to allow for parts of you to feel unheard and sabotage the work you have been doing toward living a fiercely authentic life based in love.

Allow yourself the time you need, move through your process, and reach out for additional support to help you. Take as long as you need for all parts of you to feel loved and heard and accepted. You can't rush the process of forgiveness.

THE GIFTS AND THE LESSONS

Not all relationships must transition to an end. Some transitions mean you end up staying in the same relationship or the same job, or maintaining relationships in your family. A transition doesn't mean someone leaves your life forever. Sometimes it means the relationship itself is transformed into one based in fierce love, care, authenticity, and communication.

A Course in Miracles calls that the healed relationship: the relationship in which you have rubbed each other's mirrors, tumbled with each other through the rough times, and come out the other side transformed, both of you with love in your hearts, making decisions from that space of love, care, and being in alignment with who each of you truly are. But sometimes the lesson is in learning when to walk away.

There's healing in the learning. That's where the gifts are. It's about recognizing "this happened *and* I can learn a lesson." It's less about, "This happened *so that* I can learn a lesson." When you focus on the "and," you allow yourself to access the feelings associated with each experience. When you focus on the "so that," you keep those feelings at bay.

The gift is the magical part of the journey, where you get to look back and see, despite all the experiences you have lived and all the completed relationships, the beauty in it all. One helpful practice to connect you with this beauty is an inventory of your relationships. List out all of your relationships and identify the gifts of each one.

LOVING KINDNESS MEDITATION

Sometimes, despite all of the support you have to help you heal, you will still have an extremely difficult time with identifying the lessons and being compassionate toward some individuals. That's where the Loving Kindness Meditation comes in. That boss you're still having a hard time being compassionate toward? Loving Kindness Meditation. That kid in high school who you believe ruined your life? Loving Kindness Meditation. The boyfriend or girlfriend who ripped your heart out and tore it to shreds? Loving Kindness Meditation. This is the answer on the path to helping you heal.

Loving kindness can seem like a tall order when you

are in pain and want nothing to do with the person who has hurt you, or when you're trying to navigate a transition with someone. The Loving Kindness Meditation is a paradox to help you navigate these difficult relationships. It also opens you up to receive more love.

The Loving Kindness Meditation, also known as the *metta* meditation, comes from the Buddhist tradition and is one of the most-powerful exercises in cultivating compassion for yourself and for others. What makes this exercise even better is you get to be part of it. When doing *metta* meditation, you are the first person to receive your own love and kindness. This creates the fertile soil for you to feel love and kindness, which you then ripple out to the rest of the world, including the people with whom you struggle. The *metta* meditation is, in a sense, a practice of fierce authenticity, demonstrating fierce love for yourself, then sharing it with others.

Loving Kindness Meditation isn't just for when you're having a difficult time relating with others or are trying to find peace in a situation. The practice of *metta* is recommended as a daily practice to cultivate love toward yourself and eventually to ripple love and kindness out to the world as a whole. The goal of Loving Kindness Meditation is to evoke a feeling of warm-heartedness toward the self and others. The world today greatly needs huge doses of love and kindness.

Here's how it's done: Start by getting into a comfortable seated position, typically with your feet flat on the floor and your back upright. Take a few deep breaths, focus your attention on your heart space, and begin the practice. Start by sending loving kindness to yourself, then ripple out to others, starting with those closest to you and ending with all beings on earth. Simple!

There are various ways to engage in the Loving Kindness Meditation. I'll share two versions with you: the short form and the long form. I'll start with the long form, and then give you the short form. You can consider one as a longer daily practice and one as a shorter, spot-check practice.

As you begin this practice, you might experience the opposite of the desired effect. Practicing Loving Kindness Meditation can sometimes bring up everything unlike itself, such as anger, resentment, hurt, pain, guilt, and shame. If you allow yourself to stay present with yourself throughout the exercise, you will be able to make your way past the discomfort and experience the benefits of the love and kindness, regardless of whether you consciously know it or not. The Loving Kindness Meditation is an exercise that works on the subconscious level.

The Long Form

As you focus your attention on the space at your heart, recite the following phrases to yourself, about yourself:

> *May I be happy. May I be well. May I be safe.*
> *May I be peaceful and at ease.*

Keep repeating the phrases to yourself for a period of time and notice whether you are able to connect with a warm-hearted feeling. Some people have a hard time connecting with themselves, so they like to picture themselves as children while they are sending loving kindness toward themselves.

Once you have focused on yourself for a period of time, begin to ripple loving kindness out to others, starting with those closest to you, then move out from there. After focusing on yourself, shift to those you love. Call to mind a person whom you love and care for deeply, then direct the loving kindness to them:

> *May you be happy. May you be well. May*
> *you be safe. May you be peaceful and at ease.*

Repeat this for a period of time, sending them loving kindness, then shift your attention to the next layer of the circle—a neighbor, an acquaintance, or someone about whom you are neutral:

> *May you be happy. May you be well. May you be safe. May you be peaceful and at ease.*

After repeating that for a period of time, move out one level further, calling to mind someone you have difficult feelings or a difficult relationship toward:

> *May you be happy. May you be well. May you be safe. May you be peaceful and at ease.*

If you notice resistance or sadness, grief, or other feelings other than loving kindness, know that you aren't alone. This is the layer that often brings up the most-difficult emotions as part of your emotional detoxification. You don't have to judge whatever is arising. In fact, if feelings of sadness or grief arise, it might mean your heart is softening up just a little bit, which will allow the healing to happen on a deeper level.

Again, there is no need to judge it either way. Simply stay with yourself throughout the experience.

Finally, after repeating the previous phrase for a period of time, think of all beings on this planet and repeat:

> *May all beings be happy. May all beings be well. May all beings be safe. May all beings*

be peaceful and at ease.

As you begin to wrap up the practice, allow the feelings of loving kindness to wash over you, permeating through every single cell of your body. Once you complete the practice, go about the rest of your day as usual. Notice what shift this practice has made for you.

The Short Form

The short form, or spot-check, version is for when you need to send out some loving kindness in the moment.

Take a deep breath. Connect with your heart space, and say:

May I be happy. May those I love be happy. May those I am neutral with be happy. May those I have difficulty with be happy. May all beings be happy.

May I be well. May those I love be well. May those I am neutral with be well. May those I have difficulty with be well. May all beings be well.

May I be safe. May those I love be safe. May

*those I am neutral with be safe. May those I
have difficulty with be safe. May all beings
be safe.*

*May I be peaceful and at ease. May those I
love be peaceful and at ease. May those I am
neutral with be peaceful and at ease. May
those I have difficulty with be peaceful and at
ease. May all beings be peaceful and at ease.*

If you feel you need an even-shorter spot check, such
as when you have only 2 seconds to stop yourself from an
explosion, pick one of the above phrases and use that as
your focal point. If you prefer, you can try this one on for
size, too:

Bless them. Change me.

It works.

You are also welcome to create phrases that replicate
these general ideas, as long as they are focused on cultivating warm-hearted feelings between you and others, and to
ripple those feelings of warmness, love, and kindness out
into the world.

You may have had horrible experiences at the hands of
people you may not be willing to include in your Loving
Kindness Meditation. That's okay. There's no wrong way to

do this exercise. If it feels right, start with difficult people who have caused smaller hurts than the big hurt. As you notice a softening there, and as you continue to do your healing work, the idea of including the person who caused you the big hurt may start to seem more and more appealing. You might even be surprised to find that your subconscious brain pops them into your meditation one day.

Why? Because by that point, you will no longer wish to carry the pain of the big hurt with you any longer. You will wish to free both yourself and the other people involved with the big hurt, so all of you can be released from the pain and suffering you have been carrying around within you.

This exercise works well because it not only shifts your perspective from one of fear to love, allowing you to shift the way you navigate the world, it also shifts the energy of the world in general. We are all connected. When you think or feel something toward someone else, at some level, they know it. And that affects the way you interact with them.

When met with coldness, most of us respond with coldness. However, when we can respond with warmth, our perspective of the world changes. One person has an impact on another person with their warmth, who affects another, who affects another. Before you know it, a day that could have been filled with nasty cold walls and fear-based stories and defenses becomes a beautiful day filled with love and kindness toward yourself and others. Give it a try and see for yourself what happens.

CREATING THE SPACE FOR MIRACLES

My kids respect me.

My boss doesn't get under my skin.

I moved to an amazing new job that is so right for me!

I was able to leave my partner and my world didn't come crashing down to an end.

My husband and I are finally deeply connected and our relationship is better than it's ever been.

I found a love I never knew I had, and it's been living inside me this whole time.

I never imagined this great big miraculous life was meant for me.

These are the words of the women you met as you journeyed through this book with me—women who have taken the steps suggested in this book, who looked at themselves with rigorous honesty, dove into the depths of their souls and their psyches, sat in some very uncomfortable places, allowed themselves to evaluate the gifts and the lessons in every experience, and released them all with love.

These are the women who have gone before you and have experienced the miracles that occur from doing the work required to shift their perspective from fear to love. These are the words of the women who are fiercely living and loving in their lives today.

When you embarked upon this journey with me, I told you the work would be difficult at times, and the end result would be worth it: Living and loving in an entirely new way—a way that is beyond your wildest dreams. The women who have gone before you, me included, have all been able to receive the gifts from practicing fiercely authentic love for themselves, fierce care of themselves, fiercely tuning into what is right and true for themselves, and then fiercely navigating the world from the highest expression of themselves. The gifts of love, care, kindness, compassion, vulnerability, authenticity, and fierce communication of your truth are available to you, too. The world has a limitless supply of these wonderful and beautiful resources. All you have to do is clear away the blocks that keep them from coming to you.

The work you have begun through this book has helped

you begin clearing the path through the overgrown weeds. You have created the space for miracles in your life. Miracles always surround you: You simply need to wake up to their presence. In every moment, you have the power to choose. Will you choose to focus on the story of your wound and continue to live your life by operating from the place of fear, lack, and scarcity? Or will you focus on the story of your healing, your resiliency, your beautiful journey?

Only you get to decide how you will live your life.

Do you choose to focus on the lesson and the gift in each experience? Or do you choose to focus on reinforcing the false and limiting beliefs you used to have about yourself? You are the creator of your reality. The experiences you have lived and the people who agreed to help you live those experiences have all been for your journey and your evolution. By doing the work to clear the dust, clean the grime, and Windex yourself to a bright shine, you get to return home to the truth of who you are: A beautiful spark of divine light and love; a being here to experience love, joy, freedom, and ease in your life and to share that joy, freedom, and ease in the lives of those you touch.

You aren't meant to live in chaos and struggle. You are meant to live a full life, free from toxic fear, free from drama, free from the grips of trauma, and free from the internal strife you experience when you live from your wounds. You experience your wounds so you may experience freedom from them.

By honoring transitions, practicing loving kindness, and choosing to remain connected with the gifts, you make room for new experiences to enter into your life. Experiences that are based in alignment with the fiercely authentic you, the you who you are when you are free from the pain and the wounds of your past. That's where you will receive the most-rewarding and fulfilling gifts in your life.

I know it is possible for you to experience this. Stay true to who you are, do the work, stay present with yourself even when you want to say, "Fuck this, I give up," and allow yourself to acknowledge the little miracles along the way. Little by little, the small miracles add up. One day, you will awaken with a whole new perspective on life. That day is closer than you believe.

Thank you for being here with me. Thank you for being here with you. Thank you for doing the work to honor yourself, so you can go out into the world and ripple more love and kindness onto this planet. Thank you.

Welcome to the Revolution

Grant that I may not so much seek ...
to be loved as to love.
—Prayer of Saint Francis

Fierce authenticity is a movement. It is a revolution in the way you love, work, and play. It is a movement to bring more love and more joy into a world that has let stories of unworthiness cloud the truth of how lovable and worthy we are as human beings.

You are now part of this powerful movement.

When I began developing the practice of fierce authenticity in my own life, I had no idea I was trailblazing a revolutionary way of living and loving that I would then be sharing with the world. Based on what you now know about the practice of fierce authenticity, I hope you agree that our world needs more of it. The world we live in today operates from a thought system based in fear. We need more than anything a drastic shift into a thought system based in love. By doing the work and cultivating your own practice of fierce authenticity, you are now part of the revolution, the movement, to bring more love into the world. As you have probably learned through your experience of cultivating fierce authenticity by now, the more you show up with love for yourself, the more you can show up with love for others. The more you allow yourself to be seen, the more you can see others. And the more you allow yourself to show up and be seen, the more you allow yourself to get and give love.

All any of us want at our core is to know that we are loved and accepted as we are, and that we belong. Through cultivating the practice of fierce authenticity in your life, you have begun to clear the blocks and the barriers that have prevented you from experiencing the love that has been present in your life all along. As much as it may have seemed that this work was about you learning how to get more love, the reality is that the work is about you learning how to be love so you can give more love.

When you learn how to love yourself from a fiercely authentic place in your heart and soul, you are able to give more love to others in a way that is aligned in the highest nature for us all. When you are able to give more love to others, that love not only radiates out into the world; it is returned back to you many fold. Although you may have thought this entire time that the practice of fierce authenticity was all about you, the reality is that the practice of fierce authenticity is for the betterment of the world.

Take a moment to honor yourself for being here and doing this work. It takes a tremendous amount of courage and perseverance. I invite you to pause, turn inward, connect with yourself deep in your core, and bow to yourself in reverence for following through on the work you committed to do.

The practice of fierce authenticity, although a simple process, isn't an easy process. The practice of fierce authenticity entails looking at yourself through the lens of rigorous honesty. It means getting real with yourself about where you have been mentally, emotionally, or spiritually hurt, and taking ownership of the ways you continued to perpetuate, or perpetrate, your hurt in your life.

It can be painful to take ownership of the ways in which you participated in abandoning yourself because you were acting, or reacting, based on the stories of your wounding. Yet, as you take ownership of your part in your own story, you take back parts of yourself you had given away to others. You experience the miracles of taking back ownership of your power and everything else that is rightfully yours. You experience the miracles of shifting your perspective from fear to love.

As you follow each part of the practice and stay present with yourself through your process, you are further initiated as a warrior in the revolution of bringing more love into this world through the practice of fierce authenticity. With each courageous repetition of each question for reflection and each repetition of each meditation as part of your daily practice, you further allow yourself to experience the gifts of more love, more happiness, more joy, and more connection in your relationships and your life.

As a warrior in the revolution of fierce authenticity, you demonstrate courage, commitment, dedication, and search for deep inner and spiritual truths. As a warrior in the revolution of fierce authenticity, you get love by learning how to give love: to yourself, first and foremost, and then to others around you, based in alignment with what is right and true for you. As a warrior in the revolution of fierce authenticity, you know how to fiercely love and care for others, because you have cultivated fierce love and care for yourself. Your cup is overflowing and you have love to give the world— not so the world can validate your enoughness, but so you can go out into the world and spread the message of hope and love to others who need it, too.

You have crossed the threshold.

There's no going back.

You are a warrior.

Welcome to the revolution.

It's time.

The world is ready for you to heal, so that she herself can be healed.

I bow to honor you and your commitment to spread more love in the world.

Now go forth, show up, get seen, and be love.

To take what you began here and access even deeper healing in the fierce authenticity movement to create more love in your life and the world, please visit www.fierceauthenticity.com to learn more.

FURTHER RESOURCES

Use these further resources as a guide to help you connect with support on your path towards fierce authenticity.

Community Groups for Support

RECOVERY GROUPS:

12-Step Programs: If you struggle with any of these issues, consider which support system might be of help. It is suggested that you try at least six different meetings before deciding whether a given program or group within a program is right for you.

Alcoholics Anonymous (AA): for people who have a desire to stop drinking. www.aa.org

Al-Anon: for people who have been affected by someone's drinking. www.al-anon.org

Narcotics Anonymous (NA): for people who have a desire to stop using drugs. www.na.org

Nar-Anon: for families and friends who have been affected by someone else's drug use. www.nar-anon.org

Marijuana Anonymous (MA): for people who have a desire to stop using marijuana.

www.marijuana-anonymous.org

Overeater's Anonymous (OA): for people who have a desire to stop their overeating behavior. www.oa.org

Co-Dependents Anonymous (CoDA): for people who have a desire to stop their codependent behavior.

www.coda.org

Sex Addicts Anonymous (SAA): for people who have a desire to stop their sexual addiction.

www.saa-recovery.org

S-Anon: for people who have been affected by someone else's sexual behavior. www.sanon.org

Sex and Love Addicts Anonymous (SLAA): for people who want help with their sex and love addiction or avoidance. www.slaafws.org

ALTERNATIVE RECOVERY PROGRAMS

Self-Management and Recovery Training (SMART Recovery): for people who want to abstain from their addictions. www.smartrecovery.org

Refuge Recovery: Buddhist-inspired path to recovery from addiction. www.refugerecovery.org

SOCIAL COMMUNITIES

Meetup: for getting out and connecting with people who share similar interests, with groups ranging from book clubs to hiking groups, to happy hours, and everything in between. www.meetup.com

ONLINE COMMUNITIES

Facebook Groups: let you connect online with people all over the world who share similar interests. Simply search using your area(s) of interest.
www.facebook.com

Fierce Authenticity Facebook Group: A private community for our very own Fierce Authenticity Warriors who are showing up, being seen, and opening themselves up to getting love every single day. ☺

www.facebook.com/groups/fierceauthenticity

ADDITIONAL READING

A Return to Love: Reflections on the Principles of "A Course in Miracles" by Marianne Williamson

Attached: The New Science of Adult Attachment and How it Can Help You Find—and Keep—Love by Amir Levine and Rachel S.F. Heller

Codependent No More: How to Stop Controlling Others and Start Caring for Yourself by Melody Beattie

Daring to Trust: Opening Ourselves to Real Love & Intimacy by David Richo

Facing Love Addiction: Giving Yourself the Power to Change the Way You Love by Pia Mellody

Getting the Love You Want by Harville Hendrix

The Gifts of Imperfection: Let Go of Who You Think You're Supposed to Be and Embrace Who You Are by Brene Brown

The New Rules of Marriage: What You Need to Know to Make Love Work by Terrence Real

You are the One You've Been Waiting For: Bringing Courageous Love to Intimate Relationships by Richard Schwartz

SUGGESTIONS FOR HOW TO PICK A THERAPIST OR MENTOR

When picking a therapist or mentor, the most important element is your comfort and connection with them. Healing occurs in relationships, so when you pick someone who isn't a good fit for you, it's going to be difficult to make progress with them. Here are some key considerations when choosing a therapist or mentor.

1. Ask family, friends, or other trusted people if they have a therapist or mentor they have enjoyed working with.

2. Do internet research about people you are interested in potentially working with, or do a Google/Yelp search for therapists in your area. Do they seem to have a good understanding of what you are going through? (If you are using these suggestions to find a 12-step sponsor, look for someone who has what you want. In meetings, do they share about the recovery you

hope to have one day?)

3. Call those who seem like a good fit and feel them out on the phone. Do you connect with them well enough and do you feel comfortable with them?

4. Schedule an appointment for an initial visit in person to further assess whether it feels like a good fit. (If looking for a sponsor, meet them for coffee to get to know them a little better.)

5. Be sure to show up for your scheduled appointment. Healing can't begin if you aren't showing up for it!

Picking a therapist or mentor can be a vulnerable experience. You have admitted that you need help and are open to welcoming it in. That isn't easy. Follow the steps above, call around, and choose the person who seems as if they understand you and your situation the best. Then, be prepared to let the healing begin.

ACKNOWLEDGMENTS

First and foremost, all thanks go to God, without whom the work that I do in this world would not be possible. Thank You for giving me the courage and the wisdom to show up and be of service every day. Thank You for guiding me and for showing me that Your will for me always works out better than my own.

Thank you to my parents, without whom I would not be the woman I am today. Although it felt hard growing up, I would not have it any other way. Thank you for loving me, supporting me, and cheering me on, even when the stories of my childhood clouded the inner vision of my mind.

Thank you to my sister for being the one to always remember the good times, especially when I was too caught up in the stories of my wound. I'm proud of the woman you are today and I'm so lucky to be with you again in this lifetime.

Thank you to all of the therapists, mentors, healers, coaches, and sponsors who have supported me through some of my most-challenging and painful times as I learned to cultivate the practice of fierce authenticity in my own life. Special acknowledgments to my first therapist, Dania, who had the patience to support me while I was young and naïve; to Edie, who was the first to mention the rooms of recovery to me; to Ama, for supporting me through some of the deepest depths of my healing journey; to Keri, for her unwavering love, support, and belief in me and for planting all the right seeds—for seeing me—and for her amazing wordsmith abilities; to Gitanjali, for not only teaching me about the power I hold, but also for being one of the powerful space-holders and healers who helped me evolve and grow; to Liza for the incredible family constellations work she has supported me through; to Dr. B, for being the best chiropractor and helping heal my physical body; to A'nna, for teaching me what it looks like to make the conscious decision to love unconditionally; and to Suzie, for mentoring me through what it means to be an equal partner in a partnership, especially when things get hard.

Thank you to my friends for cheering me on and sharing your experiences, strength, and hope with me, especially when things looked quite bleak and rough. Special thanks to my sisters in Keri's Sacred Soul Circle and to Alyssa, Angelic, A'nna, Anne, Debbie, Emily, Eryka, Jill, Jillian, Katie, Kerstyn, Laura, Linda, Liza, Sarah, Shannon, and Shelby. With each of you, I get to practice what it looks like to show up, be seen, and get love every single day. Thank you for being my safe people with whom I get to practice being fiercely authentically me.

A special thank you to my friends Tina and Sabrina at Enchantations in Campbell, CA for seeing in me what I was not yet able to see. Thank you for opening up your shop to me so that I could give talks and workshops, and further cultivate the message of fierce authenticity.

Thank you to my clients, who continue to show me the courage it takes to show up and be seen every single day. You are amongst the original warriors of fierce authenticity. Thank you for trusting me.

Thank you to the various editors who have helped me along with way, including early editors Christian de Quincey, Simone Grahm, and copyeditor Ruth Thaler-Carter. A special thank you to Sheila Buff for taking my words and turning them into a powerful book with a message to help heal our world; and to my designers, Amier (WildEagles99) and Roseanna White Designs for their incredible design skills and patience with me while we put the finishing touches on this book.

And lastly, thank you to the amazing man I am choosing to share my life with, who is choosing to share his life with me, too. Thank you for helping me to develop and learn the practice of fierce authenticity. Without your part in my story, the practice of fierce authenticity would not be here today. Thank you for loving me, supporting me, and being the most-perfect man on this planet for me. I love you.

ABOUT THE AUTHOR

S hirani M. Pathak is a licensed psychotherapist, spiritual teacher, energy healer, and inspirational speaker with one mission: to help bring more love into a world that is overrun with pain and fear.

Shirani is the founder of the Center for Soulful Relationships, where she provides relationship therapy to women and couples who are struggling to maintain love, connection, and intimacy in their relationships. She has a special brand of therapy where she meets with individuals and couples for private multi-day retreat-style sessions to help them get in touch with their stories, their pain, their blocks, and their fears, and learn how to re-connect with themselves and their loved ones so they can experience love and joy in their lives again.

Shirani founded the Fierce Authenticity movement (#fierceauthenticity and #showupbeseengetlove on social media) as a way to help more people learn the practice of showing up, being seeing, and getting the love they desire in their lives. She facilitates an online workshop helping women deepen into the practice, and is available for speaking opportunities.

Shirani works, loves, and plays her fiercely authentic life in San Jose, CA with her beloved (the man she knew she was meant to marry) and their dog, Benji.

To learn more about Shirani, visit
www.ShiraniMPathak.com.

Welcoming in More Support

After reading this book are you left with the feeling of wanting more? More content, more support, more exercises to help you further cultivate the practice of showing up, being seen, and experiencing love?

If you're ready for more, I invite you to join me as I lead groups of women through a guided online workshop about how to deepen into the practice.

In these online workshops, you'll go through a step-by-step process of further uncovering the stories you have, how they are hindering you, and what you can do to implement change.

To learn more, visit www.fierceauthenticity.com.